ESSENTIAL VOLUNTEER MANAGEMENT

BY STEVE McCURLEY AND RICK LYNCH

A DIRECTORY OF SOCIAL CHANGE PUBLICATION

ESSENTIAL VOLUNTEER MANAGEMENT
Steve McCurley and Rick Lynch

Published by the Directory of Social Change, Radius Works, Back Lane, London NW3 1HL (071-284 4364).

First published in USA as Essential Volunteer Management, 1989, by VM Systems and Heritage Arts Publishing. This edition fully revised. First UK publication.

ISBN 1 873860 62 5

British Library Cataloguing in Publication Data
A catalogue record for this book is available from the British Library.

Designed and typeset by Kate Bass
Printed and bound by Page Bros., Norwich

FOREWORD

Managers of volunteers have a unique role that involves a larger variety of tasks and calls upon an even larger range of skills. Often the job of the manager is under-valued or under-appreciated by the very organisation that benefits from the involvement of valuable volunteers. Why does this happen? Because the manager is working with people who are not paid? Is it because sometimes the volunteers are deemed unnecessary or inefficient, or at worst, a time-consuming exercise?

Rick Lynch and Steve McCurley's book, **Essential Volunteer Management** approaches the daunting task of managing volunteers in a systematic and thorough way, calling upon years of experience and incorporating appropriate theories respected in the field. It is an inclusive resource that takes the reader through the important aspects of managing a volunteer programme, step-by-step, issue by issue and great idea to greater idea!

In the short term, the information will highlight the basic concepts involved in dealing with volunteers. Have you thought about just WHY your organisation involves volunteers in the first place? What are the trends in the voluntary sector both in the UK and in the USA? Who are the 'new volunteers?' How and why should staff be involved in the development of a volunteer programme? What is important in the designing of jobs for volunteers? What are the secrets of a successful recruitment strategy? Why bother to interview? How can we KEEP volunteers once we've got them? How can we supervise them so that they will stay? How do we gain support for our programme and attract attention for the vital role of our volunteers? All good questions! Read the book to find the answers.

The book can also be seen with a much bigger picture in mind. At a time when many organisations are struggling with reduced resources and increased demand on services, the important question is, *'which of these many organisations will be around in the 21st Century?'* While the immediate temptation is to lobby funders for more money, to advertise for hordes of new volunteers, some to raise those much-needed funds, it may be more prudent to apply the suggestions and lessons from this book, before any drastic measures are implemented.

Which will be the successful organisations of the next century? They just may be the ones who have taken the time and allocated the necessary resources to formulate a long term strategy for the development and management of a complete volunteer programme. They are the ones who will attract volunteers, and keep them.

Anne Green
Deputy Chair, Volunteer Centre UK
and Director, Spiral Associates

ABOUT THE AUTHORS

Steve McCurley

Steve McCurley is well known in the US as a trainer and speaker in the field of effective volunteer management. He is currently a partner in VM Systems, a management consulting firm.

Each year he gives workshops to over 15,000 participants from groups as diverse as the American Hospital Association, the Fraternal Congress of America, Special Olympics International and CBS, Inc. He is the author of more than 50 books and articles on non-profit management. He is a former board member of the Association for Volunteer Administration.

Steve was born in Georgia, attended the University of Georgia and the Northwestern University School of Law, and now lives in the Washington, DC area.

Rick Lynch

With more than fifteen years' experience in the management training field, Rick Lynch is known for his ability to help organisations discover practical action to make themselves and their organisations immediately more effective. An entertaining and dynamic speaker, he has been acclaimed across North America as one of the top seminar leaders by businesses, non-profit organisations, schools and government institutions.

A frequent contributor to professional journals, he is also the author of the popular and thought-provoking book, Precision Management.

Rick is currently President of Lynch Associates, a consulting firm located in Seattle, WA.

Acknowledgements

The publishers would like to thank Anne Green, Sue Warner, Marie Tatum and Joyce Hodgkinson for their invaluable help.

CONTENTS

Chapter 1   An introduction to Volunteer
Management **1**

Chapter 2   Planning for a Volunteer
Programme **15**

Chapter 3   Creating Motivating
Volunteer jobs.................... **25**

Chapter 4   Recruitment....................... **39**

Chapter 5   Screening & Interviewing...... **68**

Chapter 6   Orientation & Training.......... **79**

Chapter 7   Supervision...................... **90**

Chapter 8   Retention & Recognition........ **115**

Chapter 9   Volunteer - Staff relations **135**

Chapter 10   Some final suggestons **155**

Appendix A   Sample Policy on
volunteer management......... **157**

Appendix B   Sample Forms to be used in
volunteer management......... **169**

Appendix C   Bibliography...................... **185**

Further reading **192**

Further information... **195**

ABOUT THIS BOOK

Essential Volunteer Management is an examination of the methods developed in the United States for operating a successful volunteer programme. It is designed to explain the approach that has made the American volunteer community one of the largest and most creative in the world. The publishers who have commissioned this book for publication in the UK feel that many of the techniques that have been developed in the United States are simply ones that reflect a need to adjust the techniques of involving volunteers to the changes that societies and their members are experiencing – rapid growth in the number of voluntary organisations, increased complexity in personal lives, multi-diversity of population groups, etc.

Topics covered include:

◆ **An overview of volunteering in both the UK and US**

◆ **Reasons for volunteering**

◆ **Changing styles of volunteers - and their implications**

◆ **Introduction to volunteer managament and the role of the programme manager**

Since these factors are worldwide, it was felt that a review of the volunteer management approach in the United States might be of use to volunteer programme managers in the UK and other areas that are undergoing the same types of changes and stresses.

AN OVERVIEW OF VOLUNTEER ACTIVITY

Volunteering in the United States

Volunteering has long been a pervasive tradition in American history. Since the days of Alexis de Tocqueville, commentators have noted the American penchant for forming voluntary groups of citizens to work on mutual problems and interests.

Currently, volunteering is one of the most commonplace activities in American society. During the 1980's and 1990's the level of volunteering has stayed at around *50% of the adult population.* In a survey conducted by the Gallup Poll organisation in 1991, almost 100 million adults reported having volunteered during the year, contributing a total of over *20.5 billion hours of their time.*

These volunteers come in all shapes, ages and sizes. With almost half of the population engaged in volunteering, it should not be surprising that the 'typical' volunteer can be almost anyone. Volunteering stretches across all age categories, with the largest amount of volunteering being done by those between ages 30-45.

◆ Volunteering in the US is *non-gender related*, with almost equal percentages of involvement of males and females.

◆ The typical volunteer donated *4.2 hours per week* to volunteering.

The recipients of these hours are equally varied. Most of the volunteer time donated was given by those engaged in formal volunteer work for organisations. About 70% of total time went to *non-profit organisations*; 20% went to *government organisations*; and 10% went to *for-profit organisations* (mostly hospitals and nursing homes).

Overall distribution of volunteering by age category in the US is as follows:

◆ 48% of those 18-24

◆ 53% of those 25-34

◆ 61% of those 35-44

◆ 56% of those 45-54

◆ 49% of those 55-64

◆ 42% of those 64-74

◆ 27% of those 75+

Volunteering by employment category:

◆ 67% of those full-time self-employed

◆ 59% of those part-time self employed

◆ 62% of those part-time employed by someone else

◆ 57% of those full-time employed by someone else

◆ 43% of those not employed

The importance of volunteers to these organisations can scarcely be over-stated. For non-profit organisations, volunteers can often make the difference between remaining in operation or being forced to close. In some ways volunteers are as important to charitable causes as are donations of money – in 1991 the estimated value of donated volunteer services was *$176 billion*. The hours donated by volunteers in 1991 represented the equivalent of *9 million full-time employees*.

Volunteering in the United Kingdom

Volunteering is gaining a higher profile in the UK with more people becoming aware of opportunities. The recent economic recession has also heightened interest with voluntary organisations now looking to increase volunteer involvement, and volunteering is very much on the political agenda. The 1992 General Election brought renewed commitment from the main political parties and in March 1994 the government's 'Make a Difference' programme was launched to increase individual involvement in the community.

According to the 1991 UK National Survey of Volunteering Activity, commissioned by The Volunteer Centre UK, up to *23 million adults* are involved in volunteering each year. The report confirms that volunteering appears to be on the increase but the growth of volunteering since 1981 has been uneven and has been concentrated in organisations concerned with sport and exercise or the environment. There has been no apparent growth in the welfare field.

To summarise some of the key findings:

◆ 51% of people over 18 had volunteered at least once in the past year, 31% at least once a month, and 22% in the previous week.

◆ 75% had been involved in informal community activity.

◆ There had been an overall increase in formal volunteering from 44% in 1981 to 51% in 1991.

◆ Over 65% of volunteers interviewed said that their volunteering could have been better organised with 1 in 4 saying that their efforts were not always appreciated and the same number saying that volunteering took up too much time. Many volunteers stated that they were dissatisfied with the tasks they were given to do.

◆ One third of volunteers said they sometimes found themselves out of pocket.

There was little difference between men & women volunteers. The figures were more marked through age differences:

18-24: 55% **35-44:** 63% **55-64:** 45%
25-34: 60% **45-54:** 60% **65-74:** 34%
75+ 25%

Formal volunteering was found to increase with income & with educational qualifications. The following are the figures shown under employment category:

◆ Managerial/ professional.. 72%
◆ Skilled manual............... 58%
◆ Unskilled...................... 37%

The average number of hours spent volunteering during the previous week was 2.7 suggesting a total of 62m hours. Combining the figures for both formal and informal volunteering suggest a total of 100m hours.

Interestingly 68% of volunteers raised or handled money in the past year and half had been involved in organising or running an activity or event.

A recent European study confirmed that voluntary action, however, is becoming increasingly issue-based with volunteers devoting their time to specific causes.

Whilst working with volunteers therefore becomes more complex in the UK, the opportunities have also never been more promising. The fact that volunteering appears to be on the increase will be seen as encouraging by those who support an expanded role for the voluntary sector and a more pluralist approach to welfare provision. The challenge is now to harness this growth to play a supportive, supplementary role both to the state and the wider community.

REASONS FOR VOLUNTEERING

Volunteers get involved for a variety of reasons.
Among the most often cited are:

◆ *'Wanted to help others.'*

◆ *'Felt obligated to give back what I got.'*

◆ *'Sense of civic duty.'*

◆ *'Religious convictions.'*

◆ *'Want to make a difference in the world.'*

◆ *'Believed in the cause.'*

These altruistic reasons are also accompanied by some self-interest motivations:

◆ *'Wanted to gain work experience. and learn new skills'*

◆ *'Like meeting new friends and being involved.'*

◆ *'Felt I could impress my employer and show leadership.'*

◆ *'It made me feel needed.'*

◆ *'Let me experience new life-styles and cultures.'*

◆ *'Do it because my job is boring and this let me have fun.'*

Many volunteers get involved for reasons to do with their families:

◆ *'Good way to spend time with my family.'*

◆ *'Wanted to set an example for my children.'*

◆ *'Had to get involved so that my children would have the benefit of the programme.'*

◆ *'Wanted to pay back help that members of my family received.'*

A typical volunteer will experience a variety of motivations, ranging from the purely altruistic to the highly self-interested, and these motivations may change through their volunteering 'career'. They will also see their motivation vary considerably from organisation to organisation and even over time within a single organisation.

The pattern of a volunteer's connection with an organisation or cause will also vary. The 'typical' volunteer in the US is involved with two organisations at any one time, which tend to change over the years. Some volunteers, however, are dedicated to or involved with only a single cause, and often spend hundreds of hours a year working on that effort.

Volunteers also vary in the length of time they stay with an organisation. Some volunteers prefer to work with many organisations, changing from group to group within the course of a single year. Others are committed to a specific cause, remaining with that group for years or even decades.

A well-run volunteer programme attempts to develop opportunities for both styles of involvement.

CHANGING STYLES OF VOLUNTEER INVOLVEMENT

Volunteering now appears to be going through some changes related to the 'style' in which people choose to participate. In some ways we seem to be moving toward a system in which there are two distinct types of volunteers:

The long-term volunteer

This type of volunteer is probably the traditional model that most of us think of when we hear the word 'volunteer.'

The long-term volunteer matches the common notion of the volunteer who is dedicated to a cause or a group. Among the characteristics of the long-term volunteer are the following:

◆ *Dedication to a cause or an organisation.* The long-term volunteer has a strong sense of affiliation with the volunteer effort and is connected to it in an 'institutional' sense, i.e., considering him/herself an 'owner' of the effort. Long-term volunteers often have a strong personal psychological investment in their volunteer role and in the sense of personal worth and identity they gain from their participation.

◆ The long-term volunteer is commonly recruited in one of two ways: By *'self-recruitment'* (finding the organisation on their own because of an already existing personal commitment to the cause), by growth from within (becoming increasingly connected over time). Or by *'cloning'*, that is, being brought to the organisation because of a close connection to the existing circle of volunteers.

◆ The long-term volunteer will tend to shape their own job and the duration of their work, adapting their time and energies to whatever is necessary to make the cause succeed. Long-term volunteers tend to be 'generalists,' willing to do whatever type of work is required and willing to do the work that is necessary to make the effort function but which is not always exciting or rewarding in itself.

◆ Motivation for the long-term volunteer is a matter of both 'achievement' and 'affiliation,' and often recognition is best expressed as a greater opportunity for involvement or advancement in the cause or the organisation.

Many established organisations have relied for years on long-term volunteers, designing jobs that require a steady donation of time over a prolonged period. In many cases these long-term volunteers were the actual 'creators' of the organisation for which they continued volunteering, helping found a structure which they later 'joined.'

The primary supply for this type of volunteering has traditionally been middle and upper income housewives, who have had the free time to donate, who have been able to offer steady hours and who have often utilised volunteering to give meaning and significance to their lives, making it their equivalent of a successful career.

Of course, long-term volunteers are not drawn solely from this category, and there are many unemployed, retired and lower income volunteers who contribute their time on a long-term basis.

The short-term volunteer

During the past ten years, however, a different style of volunteering has begun to develop. For purposes of comparison, this style might be called that of the *short-term volunteer*. Among the characteristics of the short-term volunteer are:

◆ A general interest in an organisation or cause, but usually not of extreme depth. The short-term volunteer is not a 'true believer' even though they support the cause. They do not usually view the organisation or their involvement as a central part of their own life.

◆ The short-term volunteer is usually actively recruited to join the organisation. This recruitment commonly happens through one of three methods:

➊ They may connect with an organisation because of a particular volunteer job in which they are interested, and it is the actual type of work that attracts them, not necessarily what the organisation will try to accomplish through that work.

➋ They may be recruited through participation in a specific event, such as a weekend sports programme or race. It will usually be the type of event that attracts them, or the social activity which it allows, and not the organisation or cause for whom the event is being conducted.

❸ Or they may be recruited by 'forced choice,' being 'asked' by a friend or employer to volunteer. Commonly they are volunteering for and because of their personal connection with the requester, not from any knowledge of, or commitment to, the organisation or cause.

◆ Short-term volunteers want a well-defined job of limited duration. They want to know at the beginning of their volunteering what exactly they are being asked to do and for how long they are committing to do it. Many short-term volunteers can be considered 'specialists,' because they are only with the organisation long enough to learn one job or are only willing to perform one kind of work. Usually the more limited the expected time commitment and the better delineated the scope of work, the easier it will be to recruit the short-term volunteer. Short-term volunteers may well volunteer throughout their lifetime, but they will tend not to remain too long with any single organisation, or they will only work on tasks which will allow them to closely control the extent of time which they donate.

◆ Motivation for short-term volunteers is a matter of recognising their personal achievement, not of recognising their status within the group. Recognition is a matter of thanking them for their contribution and allowing them to move on.

Oddly enough, an individual may be a short-term volunteer with one group and a long-term volunteer with another group.

On balance, it seems there is a clear shift occurring toward a preference for being a short-term volunteer. In attempting to cope with competing demands from work, home, leisure activities, and other possibilities for involvement, potential volunteers are more often choosing to limit their participation by changing the way in which they allow themselves to become involved.

NEW TYPES OF VOLUNTEERS
We are also confronted by totally new types of volunteers. These include:

◆ Employee volunteers
The UK is seeing a steady development in employee volunteering. The Volunteer Centre UK began work in employee volunteering in the early 1980s with the Crossover Project, encouraging volunteering in the years immediately prior to retirement and the Ashridge employee volunteering conference. In 1990 Whitbread organised a national conference for companies and published a Guide to Employee Volunteering.

In 1990 Business in the Community (BITC) began a two year campaign to promote employee volunteering as one of a number of forms of corporate community involvement. In addition, the Action Resource Centre (ARC), which was set up to promote secondment, also became interested in employees volunteering. In 1993 ARC was merged with the Employee Volunteering Campaign at BITC to form a new unit known as Action: Employees in the Community. The Volunteer Centre UK continues to offer a range of products and services for community organisations and employers interested in developing employee volunteering programmes.

Practice varies but the 'typical' employee volunteers will participate with a small group of colleagues for a few hours a month doing something quite practical. Those employees with particular professional or technical skills may also be encouraged to offer those skills where they are needed and senior managers may be encouraged to serve as trustees or management committee members which is another type of volunteering. National Westminster Bank, for example, has 1,200 of its staff serving as trustees.

In larger companies there will be an employee volunteer coordinator responsible for encouraging volunteering, finding volunteering opportunities and offering support. Some large companies offer cash awards, typically £100 or £500, to those organisations for whom their employees are volunteering. There is now an annual competition for the best company volunteering programme.

◆ Retired volunteers

Much of the expertise of the senior community has begun to be tapped in earnest. Many retired business people are recruited to assist in management of organisations. The American Association of Retired Persons has created a nationwide 'Volunteer Talent Bank' to assist groups in making use of the volunteer skills of its membership.

In the UK the Retired Action Clearing House (REACH) and Community Service Volunteers' Retired and Senior Volunteer Programme (RSVP) both encourage retired volunteering and place volunteers in suitable jobs.

The demographics of society and work show an increasing elderly population as people live longer and many people retiring or being retired before the statutory retirement age. This means there will be an increasing need to provide services to older people as the statutory social and health services become more stretched, and that there will be a larger pool of active retirees to draw upon as volunteers.

This presents a new challenge and new opportunities. Retirees can be recruited as an unpaid or expenses only second career, or attracted into traditional volunteering opportunities, or volunteer in completely new ways - such as at the University of the Third Age (U3A) where retired people run courses or classes for retired people.

◆ Alternative sentencing volunteers

There has been tremendous growth in the US in recent years in 'volunteering' that takes place as an alternative to or adjunct of criminal behaviour. Mandatory sentencing to 'community service' hours is now a regular part of sentencing for plea bargained agreements.

In the UK there is the Community Service Order. It is debatable whether this compulsory volunteering should be considered volunteering at all.

There are also 'intermediate treatment' schemes for young people at risk of offending and for young offenders. Some of these involve community service. Two national organisations promote such schemes – National Association for the Care and Resettlement of Offenders (NACRO) and Community Service Volunteers (CSV).

◆ Professional volunteers

Many associations of professionals have created active programmes to encourage, and in some cases require, members of their profession to perform community work. The accounting profession and the legal profession have been instrumental in attempting to create a culture of community involvement within their ranks. Some of this volunteering consists of performing the work of their profession on behalf of community groups or individuals.

The Institute of Chartered Accountants, the Law Society, the Society of Industrial Artists and Designers and the Royal Institute of Chartered Surveyors, for example, all encourage members to give their free time and become actively involved.

One interesting initiative in the UK is Lawyers in the Community, a scheme run by Action: Employees in the Community to encourage lawyers to serve as trustees and committee members.

◆ Episodic volunteers

These are volunteers who go from organisation to organisation, getting involved in one-off events, then moving on to other events at other organisations. They may participate with an organisation on an annual basis, contributing to running an event each year, but limiting their participation to that event. In the US there are formal groups of such volunteers, such as City Cares, who have targeted young adults as participants in these group volunteer activities. In many ways, these groups are taking the place of the traditional social clubs who have provided volunteers for many years.

◆ Transitional volunteers

Individuals who are changing lifestyles (housewives re-entering the job market, those with emotional disturbances moving back into interaction with others, those with disabilities learning new skills, etc.) have often undertaken volunteering as an activity to forge the path back into the community.

Often this transitional volunteering takes place informally, with people recognising that volunteering might be a next step for them. One interesting scheme is Working for a Charity, which provides a twenty-day volunteer assignment plus seven days of training over a three-month period for those looking for a return to work or a career change.

◆ The unemployed volunteer

Some individuals who are unemployed begin volunteering as a way of developing skills which may lead to paid employment. In some areas of the US, volunteering is a *requirement* for those who are receiving some government benefits while unemployed.

With nearly three million officially unemployed, and an increasing proportion of this total long-term unemployed, volunteering offers an alternative opportunity for involvement when work is not available. But attracting this group and making their involvement a success, not least for them, requires new thinking and new approaches. Amongst the unemployed are many who are low-skilled and who have become completely unused to work.

There has been a succession of government programmes to involve the long-term unemployed in meaningful community work. The latest is the Community Action Programme, which pays benefit plus £10 and is available to those who have been unemployed for six months or longer. Organisations such as CITE (Associates) Ltd. and Charity Action have become agents for recruiting and placing unemployed people on assignments lasting from six months to one year.

◆ Stipended volunteers

Even those who receive compensation have become a part of the 'volunteer' community. Several programmes in the US (such as the Senior Companion Program or the Foster Grandparents Program) pay small stipends to volunteers. The new National Service volunteer programme just enacted in the US will recruit 100,000 volunteers in the next three years, with each volunteer receiving both a small living allowance and a college-tuition benefit.

The idea of the 'paid' volunteer may be quite radical. But some payment may be both an incentive and a top up to their income for unemployed people (and their children) and the retired, many of whom are amongst the very poorest in our society.

Few of these types of 'volunteer' workers would have been recognised twenty years ago, and many are still startling to organisations who have not worked with them before. Recognising their different motivations and particular needs is important. Yet each simply represents a new way to enable individuals from the community to be of service to others.

IMPLICATIONS OF CHANGING STYLES & TYPES

These changes have impacted on volunteer management in several ways:

♦ They have necessitated major changes in job design and recruitment techniques. Organisations seeking volunteers have been forced to make jobs 'smaller' and more manageable and to cater more for the requirements of the volunteer, related to availability and duration. Jobs have in some cases had to become 'simpler' to meet the abilities of relatively unskilled or inexperienced volunteers, and in some cases have become more complex to match the abilities of very skilled professionals donating their time.

♦ Some organisations have encountered difficulties in adjusting to new types of volunteers, particularly when several types have been mixed together. As an example, long-term volunteers may well view short-term volunteers as 'uncaring' or uncommitted to the organisation. The lack of willingness of the short-term volunteer to sacrifice their own life to the interests of the cause can be viewed with a lack of understanding or even outright hostility by the long-term volunteer. Organisations have also encountered difficulties because their staff have equally difficult times adjusting to populations with whom they are not accustomed.

♦ To get enough long-term volunteers, who are actually more desirable, easier to manage and highly necessary for some leadership volunteer functions, organisations are having to rely more on 'promotion from within' grooming volunteers to assume more responsibilities and slowly convincing volunteers to commit to a greater donation of time. Much more effort has to be invested in each volunteer to develop their potential.

♦ Organisations are facing greater competition for all types of volunteers. Increasingly, the volunteer is in a favourable bargaining position, sought by several organisations, and able to pick among them for the situation which best meets their own needs and interests.

STYLES OF VOLUNTEER MANAGEMENT

Volunteer programmes also vary in style of operation. One might picture a continuum of programmes ranging from those which are very structured, with a high degree of permanent staff supervision of volunteers (such as a volunteer programme to aid those who are in prison) to those that are operated primarily by volunteers themselves (such as a Neighbourhood Watch programme).

While the principles of volunteer management remain the same in both styles of programme, the exact methods used will vary from the more institutional to the more personal orientation. The operational style of the volunteer programme has to fit the culture of the organisation.

The volunteer management process

Effective involvement of volunteers requires a planned and organised process similar to that required by any organisational project or effort. The process of volunteer management involves the following operations:

The descending steps on the left side of the diagram *(left)* represent the major elements involved in determining the needs for volunteers within the organisation, identifying suitable volunteers, and then creating a motivational structure which will support those volunteers. They are roughly analogous to the personnel and supervisory procedures for paid staff. The elements on the right side of the figure represent the other universes which interact with and must support volunteer personnel (the community at large, upper management of the organisation, and staff with whom volunteers will be in contact) and which therefore must be involved in the process of volunteer involvement.

VOLUNTEER MANAGEMENT PROCESS

- Needs Assessment & Programme Planning
- Job Development & Design
- Recruitment
- Interviewing & Matching
- Orientation & Training
- Supervision & Motivation
- Recognition
- Evaluation

STAFF INVOLVEMENT

MANAGEMENT SUPPORT

COMMUNITY INVOLVEMENT

All of these elements are interactive, and as in most creative management processes, rarely proceed in a totally linear fashion. During the existence of the overall volunteer programme, elements within this process will tend to recur with the addition of each new area of volunteer involvement (as new projects or areas of usage are created) and with the addition of each new volunteer (as the process is customised to the requirements of the individual). The process will also be re-enacted as new staff who interact with volunteers are taken on.

THE ROLE OF THE VOLUNTEER PROGRAMME MANAGER

The functions of volunteer management are sometimes played haphazardly by individual members of staff. Organisations which involve volunteers most effectively, however, do so as part of a coordinated volunteer programme. A systematic approach to volunteer involvement requires someone to plan and coordinate all the activities of the volunteer management process.

This does not mean that the Volunteer Programme Manager - sometimes called the Volunteer Coordinator or Director of Volunteers - supervises all the volunteers directly, although she or he may in a small organisation where volunteers work in a 'stand alone' programme. If all the volunteers work in a thrift shop, for example, they may work directly under the supervision of the Volunteer Coordinator.

Many volunteer programmes start out this way. As volunteers start to become involved in other aspects of the organisation, however, the Volunteer Coordinator quickly reaches the limits of her or his ability to supervise volunteers directly. At this point, volunteers start to work under the direct supervision of other paid staff. An accounting student, for example, might volunteer in the administrative office, supervised by the chief accountant.

The effective volunteer plays a critical role in the success of the entire organisation. When new projects or new directions arise, the role of volunteers is planned into them from the beginning. The Volunteer Coordinator helps top management identify needed expertise that will help the project succeed and works with paid staff to design volunteer jobs to meet those needs. She or he plans and coordinates a recruitment effort to find people who will find such work fulfilling enough to devote their leisure time to doing it, assists in the screening, interviewing, and selection processes, provides an overall orientation to the organisation, evaluates the success of the volunteer programme and plans recognition events.

The major role of the modern Volunteer Programme Manager is thus not working directly with volunteers, except those s/he recruits to help in these processes. Rather, s/he focuses attention on paid staff, securing top management support for volunteer efforts and helping individual staff do a good job of managing and retaining their volunteer helpers.

Not-for-profit organisations that excel in serving their clients realise they cannot ever hire enough expertise to achieve their missions fully. To succeed, they must encourage concerned people to donate their expertise just as they encourage people to provide financial support. In this, staff should value the Volunteer Programme Manager as much as they do the (usually much higher paid) fundraiser. The importance of volunteering in relation to fundraising is clear for those organisations where the value of the volunteer time is far in excess of the cash they raise and spend each year. The lack of importance given to volunteering is shown by the often unfulfilled potential of this resource whether it is being used directly to further the organisation's work or just to raise money for it.

Unfortunately, in too many organisations, the volunteer programme is regarded as an optional extra to benefit bored housewives. The role of the Volunteer Coordinator is undervalued in such organisations, and volunteers are confined largely to menial or clerical functions that are not directly related to the organisation's mission. Such organisations are overwhelmed by the problems they exist to solve, spending more and more resources chasing elusive grants and donations.

Effective organisations in the 1990's will involve volunteers in ever more significant roles. Volunteers, drawn from all walks of life and with all manner of skills, will be involved as equal partners with staff in pursuing the organisation's goals. When staff plan new efforts, they will identify needs for expertise and plan to involve volunteers to meet them. In order to accomplish this, top management must give more status, support, and resources to the Volunteer Programme Manager.

THE GEOMETRY OF VOLUNTEER INVOLVEMENT

Another way of looking at the process of volunteer management can be represented through the use of simple geometric figures *(left)*. These geometric figures illustrate what and how interacting processes of volunteer management work. Throughout this book we will be referring to these figures as a way of demonstrating what actually ought to be happening throughout the process of managing a volunteer programme.

THE GEOMETRY OF VOLUNTEER INVOLVEMENT

We will be working with three simple shapes:

The Square
Representing the process of developing jobs within the organisation.

The Circles
Representing the individual needs of the volunteer and the organisational needs of the organisation.

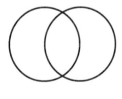

The Triangle
Representing the network of relationships among the volunteers, the volunteer manager and the organisation staff.

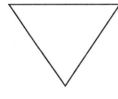

Taken together, these three shapes illustrate the major tasks which must be accomplished in order for volunteer management to be effective.

CHAPTER TWO
PLANNING FOR A VOLUNTEER PROGRAMME

An effective volunteer programme needs clear guidelines and procedures - time spent planning will limit confusion and problems later on.

GETTING THINGS STARTED

Some volunteer efforts have suffered from the problems generated by 'spontaneous creation.' This phenomenon occurs when an over-enthusiastic administrator learns of the potential of volunteer involvement and pronounces at a staff meeting: *'Let there be volunteers!'*

Topics covered include:

♦ **Getting started**

♦ **Rationale for a volunteer programme**

♦ **Staff involvement and attitudes**

♦ **Organisational climate**

♦ **Personnel policies and procedures**

♦ **Evaluation and assessment**

The assumption behind this pronouncement is that instituting a volunteer effort is simple and can be done instantaneously. The pronouncement is usually followed by the designation of some unsuspecting staff person as 'in charge of volunteers,' with the immediate assignment of 'going out and rounding up a bunch of them.'

This simple-minded approach might, in fact, work if all that is being considered is an *ad hoc* usage of volunteers, bringing in a few volunteers specifically to work with a single project, with no expectation that they will stay beyond that project or attempt to work in other areas of activity. The approach will not work at all when considered on an institutional basis: enabling volunteers and staff to work on an on-going basis in a variety of programmes and tasks throughout the organisation.

Effective volunteer management is simple in theory, but subtle in operation. It has all the complexities of basic personnel management – job development, interviewing, supervision, evaluation of performance, recognition and reward, etc. And it also has complexities all of its own. An interesting example, not seen as often in the environment of paid staff, is that of the *over-enthusiastic* worker. Quite often, volunteer managers will have to deal with a volunteer who causes difficulties for the programme not from a lack of motivation, but from a surplus of it. This volunteer will be so dedicated to the cause that they will expect and work for instant solutions to any problem that arise, and will not understand why the system sometimes operates so slowly. The volunteer may become impatient and infuriated with everyone else, paid staff or volunteers, who doesn't give total dedication to making the system work perfectly, and immediately.

Effective volunteer programmes do not happen spontaneously, and they do not happen by accident. A well-designed programme is the result of many factors, and many decisions before any volunteers are sought.

Fitting together the puzzle

In a way, one might think about volunteer management within an organisation as the construction of a puzzle. (*see diagram on left*)

Over recent years, the configurations of this puzzle have become increasingly complicated. The size of the square has increased, as organisations have developed broader uses for volunteers, involving volunteers in tasks previously reserved for paid staff. And the complexity of the job mix has changed, as organisations have developed more short-term volunteer jobs, jobs which require a lesser time commitment and greater flexibility to meet the needs and interests of the short-term volunteer.

The volunteer manager is usually responsible both for designing the overall puzzle shape and for fitting together the individual pieces that complete the puzzle. This has to be done in concert with both the staff, who help design the parameters, and the volunteers, who help determine the design of individual jobs.

FITTING TOGETHER THE PUZZLE

The overall square shape of the puzzle represents the total universe of work that the organisation desires to be accomplished through the work of volunteers.

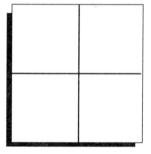

Within that square are the individual pieces of jobs that are to be done by specific volunteers, with each piece representing a volunteer.

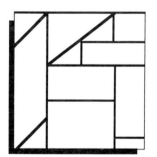

For the typical organisation today, the puzzle more closely resembles a jigsaw puzzle, one that changes shape every week.

RATIONALES FOR A VOLUNTEER PROGRAMME

The first step in constructing the design of an organisation's volunteer programme requires determining *why* the organisation wishes to involve volunteers. This decision will influence the following:

◆ It will determine the types of jobs and responsibilities that the organisation will create for volunteers.

◆ It will enable the organisation to better explain to volunteers how and why they are contributing to the work of the organisation.

◆ It will enable the organisation to explain to staff why volunteers are being sought.

◆ It will enable the organisation to develop a plan for evaluating whether the involvement of volunteers has been effective.

Reaching agreement on a rationale

It is highly desirable that some consensus agreement among organisation leadership and line staff is reached on this rationale. In a sense, the rationale will represent part of the 'mission' of the volunteer programme. It will provide a quick and clear understanding of what benefit the organisation thinks will be derived from the involvement of volunteers, and provide a sense of purpose for the volunteer programme. In essence, it should answer the question, *'why are we doing this?'*

This is important. But it is particularly important where there is or appears to be a substitution of paid work.

Potential rationales

There are many potential rationales for involving volunteers. These include:

❶ Providing an outreach to the community.

❷ Supplementing staff resources and experiences, adding value to the organisation and its work.

❸ Substituting for a paid job when the resources are simply not there to make a staff appointment.

❹ Allowing a channel for community input.

❺ Giving a more personal touch in services to clients.

❻ Building linkages to other groups.

❼ Assisting in fund-raising efforts.

❽ Cost-effectiveness in service delivery.

❾ Allowing quick reaction to changing needs or crisis situations.

❿ Responding to a request by someone to do something useful for the cause.

The consensus agreement should then be written down, and passed on to volunteers and staff. Over the page is a sample mission statement regarding volunteers used by the Juvenile Court in Spokane, Washington State.

CASE STUDY

sample mission statement from the Juvenile Court in Spokane, Washington State:

The Spokane County Juvenile Court is committed to providing the best and most appropriate services possible. To realise this goal, our Department shall make every effort to enlist the cooperation of all available resources. The Department is committed to the development of a public-private partnership which includes volunteers as an important and necessary ingredient in the development and delivery of services.

In addition to the above, our Department plans to actively implement and maintain a responsible programme of citizen involvement because:

❶ Our Department will never have sufficient resources to meet all service needs. Even if such resources were available (professional staff, finances, facilities, etc.), the Department would still believe it necessary for the community to become involved in juvenile issues.

❷ It has been demonstrated repeatedly that volunteers can significantly enhance, expand, and upgrade services. With appropriate recruitment, screening, training, and supervision, volunteers can perform almost any task effectively and responsibly.

❸ The Department feels it necessary to involve the community in the problems we are trying to alleviate or solve. Efforts to involve the community in organisation affairs will help to educate the public about these problems and will create a more enlightened and active citizenry.

Because volunteers are regarded as key members of the Juvenile Court team, their increased involvement in our Department will be pursued.

To ensure effective implementation and maintenance of citizen involvement efforts within this organisation, the following principles shall be followed:

❶ Volunteers shall be involved in the organisation's service delivery system in every unit of operation which is feasible under the laws of this State and within the scope of this Department's policies and procedures.

❷ The Volunteer Programme shall have representation at the organisation's general management and administration level. A professional staff member will be designated a Volunteer Coordinator to direct volunteer recruitment, screening, orientation, and training.

❸ Volunteers will be used in both direct and indirect services, and staff will be encouraged to utilise this valuable resource in planning programmatic activities.

❹ Professional staff and volunteers shall be involved collectively in the planning and implementation of the Volunteer Programme.

❺ The organisation shall take steps to ensure that professional staff are prepared and actively participate in implementing the Volunteer Programme. Consequently, general orientation sessions for new employees shall include information about the organisation's citizen involvement efforts, and staff shall be trained in working with and supervising volunteers. Such training shall be incorporated into the on-going organisation staff development programme.

❻ All aspects of the Volunteer Programme and its implementation will be monitored and evaluated on an on-going basis. The need to develop services that are effective, efficiently delivered and cost-effective make this a necessity.

❼ Volunteers within the organisation are not intended to replace existing professional staff. Volunteers are regarded as non-paid staff working in conjunction with professional staff to:

- ◆ Lend their skills and abilities from a unique perspective
- ◆ Amplify many areas of our Department's service to the community
- ◆ Make direct contributions to staff effectiveness
- ◆ Benefit the community at large through their added awareness of juvenile issues.

STAFF INVOLVEMENT IN PROGRAMME DESIGN

Throughout the volunteer programme design process, it is essential to involve all levels of staff. If volunteers are going to be working in conjunction with paid staff, whether for them, alongside them or in support of them, it is vital that staff are in agreement about the purpose and worth of the volunteer job and the volunteer programme as a whole.

Staff who do not want to work with volunteers can destroy a volunteer effort, either through direct opposition or through indifference. If staff are not willing to cooperate in developing realistic jobs for volunteers, if they ignore volunteers or give them second class status in the organisation, if they indicate by word or by action or inaction that volunteers are a hindrance, not a help, then volunteers will quickly become disillusioned and de-motivated, and they will quickly find other causes and other organisations with which to volunteer, or they may stop volunteering altogether.

Surveying staff attitudes

One method of assessing staff attitudes is to conduct a survey. The survey, which can be done either through personal interviewing or through a printed questionnaire, should ascertain:

1 *The level of experience of staff in working with volunteers:*

◆ Have they ever supervised volunteers before?

◆ Have they ever worked in an organisation which involved volunteers?

◆ Do they volunteer themselves?

2 *The level of comfort of staff in regard to volunteers:*

◆ Are there jobs that staff volunteers feel should not be doing? And why?

◆ Are there programme elements, such as additional staff training, which should be instituted before volunteers are brought in?

3 *Any fears that staff might have about volunteer involvement:*

◆ Are there potential difficulties, such as organisational liability or quality control questions that should be addressed?

◆ Are there worries about loss of staff jobs?

The responses to the survey should tell the volunteer manager how staff are likely to react to the inclusion of volunteers, a topic which is discussed in greater depth in the chapter on 'volunteer-staff relationships.'

Top management support

It is also desirable to have the support of the top management of the organisation. This support might be represented by the official adoption by the trustees, management committee or executive committee of the organisation of a policy supporting the use of volunteers, or by a position statement on volunteers approved by the chief staff of the organisation. One essential element of this support is that the top management and senior staff should have a clear vision of how the volunteer programme will contribute to the achievement of the organisation's mission. Some key questions that top management should consider when contemplating the creation of the volunteer programme include:

◆ How would you describe the mission of the organisation and how do you see volunteers aiding in the fulfilment of that mission?

◆ What is it at this specific time that leads the organisation to consider starting a volunteer programme?

◆ What specific goals are envisioned for the volunteer programme during its first year of operation?

◆ What kind of resources is the organisation willing to invest in involving volunteers?

◆ What type of return value does the organisation see itself getting from the involvement of volunteers?

It is important to note, however, that while it is desirable to have top management support for the involvement of volunteers, it is not desirable to have that support become coercive in nature. It is not possible for management to *compel* staff to involve volunteers. Opposing staff can too easily drive volunteers away or can too easily make it impossible for volunteers to be successful. What is desirable is an attitude by top management that encourages and rewards effective involvement by staff of volunteer resources, an approach using the 'carrot' and not the 'stick.'

ORGANISATIONAL CLIMATE

Overall organisational climate will also influence how volunteers can be involved. Volunteers will quickly become aware of overall attitudes within the organisation, whether about how well the organisation is doing, how things are done, or who and what is important to the organisation. These sometimes subtle cues regarding organisational style will influence the determination by volunteers of whether the organisation is worth the donation of their time. Since the organisation will become a work site for the volunteers, they are more likely to appreciate and stay at the organisation which has a positive environment. What is needed is a sense of common mission and purpose, and an understanding that productive steps are being taken toward the accomplishment of that mission and purpose.

An organisational climate which is favourable towards volunteers will communicate two feelings or attitudes to the volunteers:

Acceptance: The volunteers are welcomed by and connected with the overall purpose and operations of the organisation.

> Some indicators of good organisational climate include:
>
> ◆ **Clear sense of individual roles, with respect for roles of others**
> ◆ **Willingness to sacrifice for a goal**
> ◆ **Trust**
> ◆ **Tolerance and acceptance**
> ◆ **Open and honest communication**
> ◆ **Group identity: 'we're in this together'**
> ◆ **Inclusion, not exclusion**
> ◆ **Mutual support and interdependence**

Appreciation: That each volunteer has a unique, recognized contribution to make to the purpose and operations in the organisation.

PERSONNEL MANAGEMENT
Policies and procedures

Volunteer programme management also requires the creation of some formal rules and procedures. After the determination of why volunteers are to be involved, the organisation will need to develop its own set of policies and procedures governing the involvement of volunteers.

The policies will allow the volunteer manager to develop a consistent pattern of volunteering, and will provide assistance in dealing with problem situations. Both the policies, and the procedures by which they will be implemented, should be developed in conjunction with staff, particularly if the organisation is using volunteers in a variety of different types of project or activities. *Some samples of volunteer policies are provided in Appendix A.*

If you have a question about the content of a policy or procedure, refer to the organisation policies and procedures that the organisation uses for paid staff. The rules should be as similar as possible: *'when in doubt, copy.'*

Forms and records

The volunteer programme will also need to develop some basic personnel-related systems. Volunteer programmes operate with the essential forms required for any operation involving people:

◆ intake forms
◆ job descriptions
◆ contracts of 'employment'
◆ evaluation instruments

Individual records need to be maintained for each volunteer, giving:

◆ their biographical and contact information
◆ records of their positions and training
◆ hours contributed and tasks accomplished
◆ expenses claimed and reimbursed
◆ dates of connection with the organisation

The systems and files developed should match those of paid staff, and can often be the same forms.

Investigate the use of computer software packages to assist in these personnel functions. Software packages are now available (or can be custom developed for your programme) that will greatly aid you in keeping track of the names, skills, interests, and availability of your volunteers. They can help you to perform the paperwork functions of volunteer management, conserving your time to deal with those parts of the job which require human contact.

EVALUATION

The plan for the volunteer programme should also consider the process by which the volunteer's contribution is to be evaluated. The design of the programme operations should include the management information systems which will enable staff, management, volunteers, and the volunteer manager to determine how things are going and whether things can be improved on a regular basis.

The intent of evaluation is both to uncover problems (low rates of volunteer retention; need for additional training) and to reward accomplishment. Much like individuals, organisations and programmes need to know when they are successful; without measurements of what success is and when it has been accomplished, it is impossible to know when you have 'won.'

In developing the evaluation plan, consider the following questions:

❶ What would volunteers like to know about themselves, about the programme?

Hours contributed, benefits to clients, etc.

❷ What would staff who work with volunteers like to know?

Numbers of volunteers in their area, number of clients served, etc.

❸ What would top management like to know?

Who is utilising volunteers, value of volunteer time donated, etc.

❹ What would the volunteer manager like to know?

Where volunteers are coming from, rate of volunteer turnover, etc.

ASSESSING YOUR PLAN

Assess your plan for volunteer involvement by reviewing the following checklist. If you have not completed the items on the list, then you still have preparations to finish before you and your organisation can effectively involve volunteers:

◆ Have we consulted with staff who will be working with each volunteer?

◆ Are these staff clear on what their role will be in working with the volunteer?

◆ Is a complete and accurate job description written for this position?

◆ Does the position description clearly identify the qualifications for the job and outline both the purpose and nature of the work to be done?

◆ Have we identified a good working environment for the volunteer, in terms of supervisory relationships, workspace, equipment, etc.?

◆ Do we have a plan for seeking qualified applicants for the positions?

◆ Do we know how we will distinguish qualified applicants from unqualified applicants? Do we know what we will do with unqualified applicants?

◆ Do we have a plan for orienting and training this volunteer?

Operate by these rules:

◆ Think first, and get volunteers later.

They'll apreciate your consideration

◆ Do it right the first time; it's easier than having to do it over again.

Resist the impulse to quickly initiate a volunteer effort. The time spent in planning and preparation will greatly reduce both confusion and problems that arise later.

CHAPTER THREE
CREATING MOTIVATING VOLUNTEER JOBS

Before recruiting volunteers you need to have a clear understanding of the duties they are to carry out, ensuring that the roles have been clearly defined. This chapter explains the steps to producing a volunteer job description.

Topics covered include:
- **Involvement of members of staff**
- **Design of the job and level of responsibility**
- **Volunteer job descriptions**
- **Matching jobs to volunteers**

STAFF INVOLVEMENT

In an organisation employing staff, a volunteer manager should begin the process of creating volunteer jobs by gaining staff involvement. This process is one of the most important functions of the volunteer manager: without 'good' jobs, the organisation will have nothing of value to offer volunteers. Organisations that can offer interesting and productive jobs will find it easier to attract and keep volunteers than organisations with boring or unsatisfactory jobs which will have an impossible time retaining them.

Consulting with staff

The role of the volunteer manager in job development is thus one of 'consulting' with staff, so that organisational support can be provided for interesting and worthwhile jobs. During this process, the volunteer manager interviews staff to determine how best to involve volunteers. Merely asking staff what jobs they might have for a volunteer is unlikely to provoke a creative response from staff who have had no experience working with volunteers.

Instead, the volunteer manager should take staff through a process (first developed by Ivan Scheier) whereby they are encouraged to answer the following questions:

❶ *'What are the parts of your job that you really like to do?'*

Staff responses might include activities such as working directly with clients, doing research, or public speaking.

❷ *'What are the parts of your job that you dislike?'*

Responses might include compiling reports, writing the organisation newsletter, or filing.

❸ *'What other activities or projects have you always wanted to do but never had the time for?'*

Responses might include working with a new client group, investigating new sources of funding, or starting a programme in a new community.

❹ *'What would you like to see done that no one has the skills to do?'*

Responses might include upgrading the organisation's computer capability, doing market research, or creating a new organisation logo.

The answers to these questions can form the basis for defining volunteer jobs that can be integrated with the staff workload and which will be supported by staff. If the volunteer manager can find a volunteer to relieve staff of tasks they don't enjoy thereby giving them time for the things they've always wanted to do, staff have a powerful incentive to make sure that the volunteer has a good experience at the organisation. In this way the volunteer manager develops volunteer work that is both 'real' (i.e. it really needs to be done) and will be appreciated by the staff. Consequently, the potential for typical staff-volunteer difficulties, such as staff forgetting to thank volunteers for their efforts, is greatly reduced.

The interview process described here can also be used to educate staff as to the correct 'shape' for a volunteer job request, as will be discussed later in this chapter. By helping staff to develop the description of the work to be done, the volunteer coordinator will considerably lessen the prospect of being bombarded with impossible requests for volunteers: *'Someone to come in from 10-5, Monday to Friday, to do my filing.'*

CONSULTING TOOLS

The volunteer programme manager can employ a number of tools to show staff what will be possible. A 'menu' approach, giving staff lists of possibilities is often effective. The tools include:

❶ A list of the types of jobs/functions that volunteers are already performing in the organisation.

❷ A list of types of jobs/functions that volunteers perform in other organisations in the community or in similar programmes across the country.

❸ Skills/descriptions of already available volunteers.

These listings will serve to provide ideas on potential jobs to staff who might not have a clear understanding of the potential roles of volunteers within the organisation, and should broaden the perspective and improve the creativity of staff in developing interesting and challenging volunteer positions.

The circle of staff needs

The process of staff involvement should be a continuous one. The volunteer manager should develop a process for on-going communication with staff, either by periodic follow-up interviews or through written communication, in which the process of new job development continues. One method for accomplishing this is to institute a 'work wanted' section in the organisation's newsletter or via a memo to all staff, in which volunteer jobs are highlighted or in which the skills of new volunteers are announced. The aim of this communication is to create a demand for additional types of volunteer effort.

The circle represents the universe of needs and interests of the staff, formatted into a request for particular work to be done. The circle includes requests for:

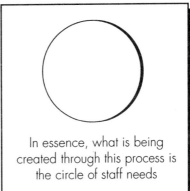

In essence, what is being created through this process is the circle of staff needs

◆ Specific skills that are needed.

◆ Time commitment that is required.

◆ Attitudes and other qualities that represent what the organisation is looking for in a volunteer.

DESIGNING VOLUNTEER JOBS FOR RESULTS

Volunteer jobs that are boring and unsatisfying, lead to rapid burnout and frequent turnover. Interesting, challenging, rewarding jobs, lead to high enthusiasm and good results from the volunteer. The difference between the two depends in part on the person doing the job; different people have different motivational needs and find different jobs interesting or boring. An often overlooked source of this difference, however, lies in the design of the job itself.

The cornerstone of all successful programmes is placing volunteers in jobs they look forward to, which should ensure stability and high morale. While paid people will do a job that is unrewarding because they are compensated for doing it, volunteers will not do so for long. This has given volunteers in general a reputation among paid people of being unreliable. On the contrary, if the volunteer does not find the job to be personally satisfying, he or she can be relied upon to leave. To attract and retain volunteers, we must design jobs they want to do.

Job descriptions of volunteers in most organisations seldom differ from those of paid staff. The jobs tend to be designed around the standard management practices of the non-volunteer world. The people who show up every day to do jobs in the paid world, however, often do so not because of a love for the work or a commitment to the cause, but out of a desire to earn a salary. When we design jobs for volunteers, therefore, we might more productively heed the principles of those who design games.

Games are voluntary activities that are designed to be intrinsically motivating. Games are so motivating, in fact, that people will spend lots of their time and money on expensive equipment and lessons in order to get better at them, something that is rarely true of work. Games are so well designed, in fact, that people will spend lots of money to get to see other people play them. If this were true of work, we wouldn't have to worry about getting funding – we could just sell tickets to watch people do their work.

The point here is not that volunteering should be a game, but that it should have the same motivational qualities that games do. All games have four characteristics that work can also have but seldom does –

❶ Ownership

❷ The authority to think

❸ Responsibility for the results of outcomes

❹ Keeping score

When we design volunteer jobs, therefore, it is good to try to maintain these characteristics. Jobs designed with these characteristics also require less supervisory effort.

❶ Ownership

By ownership, we mean that the volunteer has a sense of personal responsibility for something. Their job contains something they can point to and say *'This is mine.'* This might be a particular product or event or geographic area. In the non-profit world, the ownership is often a volunteer's own client they are helping or project they are working on. There are many examples of volunteers having such responsibility: mentors and buddies, phone workers in a crisis clinic, a companion or visitor to an elderly person, a language or literacy tutor and foster grandparents are all volunteers who have one or more clients that are 'theirs.'

Ownership is destroyed when volunteers do only one of many activities the organisation provides as part of its service. In some social care organisations, for example, volunteers might do a preliminary screening of client needs, then hand over to a trained professional who would offer specific advice or determine eligibility for services. When volunteers merely do one activity in a whole cycle, they can lose the intense satisfaction of helping others that drives most volunteer efforts. Although they know that somewhere down the line they have contributed to client's needs, their sense of pride and ownership is diluted by all the others who have had a hand in it.

Similarly, volunteers fixing up a school will tend to get more satisfaction if they do all the activities related to refurnishing a particular room than if they do one activity (such as painting or washing windows) in all the rooms. The first circumstance provides them with a sense of ownership (*'This is my room'*) whereas in the second case the sense of ownership and responsibility becomes diluted, causing such volunteers to burn out much faster than those having full responsibility for a client or a project.

> Ownership gives the volunteer something to be in charge of and hence to be proud of. Giving volunteers a project of their own that they can control is particularly important to today's new breed of volunteer, who are less interested in making a long-term commitment to an organisation than volunteers used to be. And it is also particularly important in attracting new volunteers. A 1988 study by the J.C. Penny Foundation, for example, found that 79 per cent of US citizens who do not volunteer said that the most important incentive in getting them to volunteer would be a short-term project.

This is not to say that teamwork should be avoided in job design. Teams of people can also have ownership. In this case, there is a sense that we have something that is 'ours.' In one city, for example, there is an all-volunteer programme which was formed when the parks department reduced its complement of maintenance staff as a result of a budget cut. Teams of volunteers had parks of their own which they kept free of trash and graffiti. In this case, the sense of ownership was met because the team could look at 'our park' and take pride in its appearance.

❷ The authority to think

The difference between a team and a collection of isolated individuals is that a team has the authority to plan and evaluate its work, and agree on who is going to do what. This authority to think is the second key element in good job design, whether for individuals or teams. With this authority, the individual or group not only does the work but can also play some part in deciding how to do it.

Often volunteer directors have a built-in resistance to allowing volunteers this authority. The volunteer may work only a few hours per month and so have difficulty keeping up with what is going on. Also, standard management practice holds that it is the supervisor's job to do the plan and the employee's job to carry out whatever has been decided.

Indeed, when a volunteer first comes on board, this may be the most comfortable way to proceed. As volunteers learn the job and begin to figure out what is going on, however, the fact that they are only doing what someone else decides begins to sap their motivation and dilute their feelings of pride in what they accomplish. They will tend either to resent being told what to do or to lose interest in the job. Either of these will increase the likelihood of their dropping out.

This should not mean abdicating our responsibility for ensuring good results from volunteers. Obviously, we can't afford to have all volunteers doing whatever they think is best, and without guidance. We need to make sure that they are all working toward achievement of a coordinated and agreed set of goals. What we can do, however, is involve them in the planning and deciding process so that they feel a sense of authority over the 'how' of their job.

The process of managing all this is explained in detail in the chapter on empowering volunteers. For now, suffice it to say that in designing the job we should ask:

◆　*'How would a person who tells the volunteer what to do know what to tell him?'*

Or we could ask:

◆　*'What does the volunteer's supervisor do in order to figure out what to tell the volunteer to do?'*

We can then include those thinking tasks in the volunteer's job description, healing the schism between thinking and doing. In a sense, in doing this, we give the volunteer back his or her brain.

❸ Responsibility for results

The third critical element in developing a work structure that encourages excellence is to make sure that volunteers are held responsible for achieving results, rather than simply for performing a set of activities or 'job duties.' If they are responsible for results or outcomes, they are focused on the end product of what they do, and they get the satisfaction of making progress toward a meaningful accomplishment. A crime prevention volunteer in a Neighbourhood Watch scheme, for example, will get a lot more satisfaction if responsibility for reducing burglaries with effectiveness is measured against this yardstick (insofar as is possible) than if they see the job as being knocking on doors to talk to people about planting 'hostile shrubbery' under their windows.

Most job descriptions for both volunteers and paid staff are not defined in terms of results. Instead, they merely list a series of activities the volunteer is supposed to perform. The result is never mentioned. Often, responsibility for the result is fragmented, with several people performing tasks if the result is to be achieved. In fact, the responsibility is sometimes so fragmented, that the volunteer loses sight of the result. As a direct consequence of this, results are poorly and inefficiently obtained and the volunteer gets bored.

Because it can be difficult at first to grasp the concept of defining jobs in terms of results, let's look at some examples. A volunteer in a drug abuse programme, for example, may be told that his job is to spend three hours per week counselling a client. This is a statement of an activity to be performed. No result of the counselling has been specified, and if the volunteer doesn't achieve much, we shouldn't be surprised. The job as defined requires no particular skill, other than sitting in a room with someone for three hours. To define the result, we need to ask, *'What is the outcome we want from the counselling? What should the volunteer accomplish in these three hours per week?'* The answer would probably be something like 'Clients will be able to cope with daily life without resorting to the use of drugs'. By defining this, we offer a challenging and worthwhile accomplishment for the volunteer to be working toward.

> Volunteers in a school programme might be asked to work with children on reading skills. When we ask only that someone 'work with' the children, we are not creating any responsibility for helping the children learn. There is no challenge in the job when it is defined in this way. It is better to specify the specific skill improvements that the volunteer is responsible for helping the child achieve. The result might read something like *'Bring the child's reading abilities up to age 6 reading level.'*

Defining volunteer jobs in terms of results, helps to meet people's need for a sense of achievement or accomplishment. It helps them feel that their volunteer activity is valuable and worthwhile. It also helps the volunteer programme operate more effectively. When people know what they are supposed to accomplish, they are more likely to do so. It makes sense that we should let volunteers know what results are expected and then hold the volunteers responsible for accomplishing them.

❹ Keeping score

The fourth critical element in good job design is deciding how to measure whether, and to what degree results, are being achieved. If this is not done, the statement of result will fail to have any motivating value, and it will be impossible for both volunteer and supervisor to know how well the volunteer is doing.

Many volunteer managers shy away from measuring volunteer performance, thinking that doing so would discourage or demotivate them. The opposite is more likely to be the case. If people can't tell how well they are doing, if they are succeeding or failing, they tend to get bored with the activity. There is also no incentive to try a different course of action, if you don't know that your present course isn't working.

For some jobs, the measure of performance is fairly obvious and easy to state. In the case of a crime prevention volunteer, for example, the number of burglaries in the area is a readily available statistical measure. We can use these statistics (provided the volunteer is responsible for the same geographic area for which statistics are being compiled) to measure the result of keeping people safe from burglaries. Every time a burglary occurs in the area, the volunteer will naturally ask *'what could have been done to prevent that?'* These thoughts spur creativity, and encourage new, and hopefully, even more effective approaches. If the job is merely defined as engraving personal identification numbers on people's stereos, however, and there is no feedback on how well the volunteer is doing, there will be little likelihood that more effective approaches will be tried.

In other cases, we find the measure more difficult. In the case of the Girl Guide leader whose result is to help the guides develop self-assurance, it is hard to decide how we are going to measure progress. We need to ask questions such as *'How will we know if they gain self-assurance? What would we see when they are and when they aren't self-assured? What questions could be asked to determine their degree of self-confidence?'*

Many volunteer leaders don't want to do this much work, and so they take the easy course of holding the volunteer accountable only for performing a set of activities. By doing so, however, they deprive the volunteers of the ability to tell how well they are doing. They also deprive them of a sense of accomplishment.

> ❝ **If people can't tell how well they are doing, if they are succeeding or failing, they tend to get bored with the activity.** ❞

Taking the time necessary to define how to measure volunteer progress toward results is management work. It is an essential job that all managers should engage in but many do not. In doing so, we throw away a major motivator.

Many volunteer managers who do measure performance tend to measure the wrong things. They keep track of things such as hours spent or miles driven or client contacts made. These measures tend to lack any real meaning because they do not describe whether anything of value is being accomplished or whether the result is being achieved.

To determine how to measure a given result, involve the volunteers who do the job, by asking

◆ *'What information would tell us if you are succeeding in achieving the result?'*

◆ *'How could we collect it?'*

Measuring performance makes it possible to introduce an element of competitiveness. It is possible to set targets and to encourage these targets to be surpassed, and even for the setting of records. Records are tremendously motivating. People daily do ridiculous things to break records, such as making an omelette that weighs four tons. The Guinness Book of Records lists some of these impossible achievements. If people spend time and effort to do such silly things, voluntarily, think of the productive work they might do if there were records for something more serious!

VOLUNTEER JOB DESCRIPTIONS

Each volunteer should have a written job description which should be developed jointly by the volunteer coordinator and the member of staff who will supervise the volunteer. It provides a summary of the work and activities to be performed by the volunteer, and can be used in supervision and evaluation.

The discipline of writing a good job description is useful. In some ways, job descriptions can be much more important for volunteer staff than for paid staff. Paid staff are accustomed to 'learning' their job by osmosis - coming to work and spending time watching what is happening and determining what they should be doing, how they should be working. For a volunteer, this learning period may be excessive, since ten days of on-the-job learning can easily translate into several weeks for a part-time volunteer. Unless the organisation is prepared for the volunteer to begin work immediately and has prepared suitable instructions, the volunteer can become discouraged right from the start. A job description which accurately represents the tasks to be undertaken and the effort that is required can serve as a method for readying the organisation for the appearance of the volunteer. If you discover that either you or the staff with whom the volunteer will be working cannot put together a precise job description, then it would be better to re-initiate the process of job development than to recruit a volunteer for a position which cannot be properly defined.

A good job description will contain the following elements:

Title:
What the job will be called, or what position is being offered

Purpose:
The result the job is to accomplish. This is the most important part of the job description.

Suggested Activities:
Examples of what might be done to accomplish the purpose. The word suggested indicates that the volunteer has some authority to think, to pursue other approved activities if her supervisor agrees these might be effective in achieving the result.

Measures:
How we will tell if the result is being achieved.

Qualifications:
What skills, attitudes, and knowledge are desired, as well as any requirements such as dress or conduct.

Time frame:
Estimated number of hours, length of commitment, and flexibility in scheduling.

Site:
Location of work.

Supervision:
Relationships with staff and other volunteers, reporting requirements and supervisory relationships, as well as procedures for monitoring and dealing with problems.

Benefits:
Training, insurance, parking, reimbursement of expenses, child care provision, any volunteer remuneration, events to thank volunteers, etc.

An additional item to include might be the values and philosophy of the organisation that the volunteer is expected to adhere to.

The precise format of the job description is not important. What is important is that all of the elements are covered and that, in particular, a well-thought purpose be defined for the volunteer.

CASE STUDY

There are four essential principles of a well-designed job: ownership, authority to think, responsibility for results, and keeping score. In the US, there is a volunteer programme whose main purpose is to do household chores for handicapped and elderly people who might otherwise be institutionalised. Originally, the volunteer job description wasn't even in writing. Volunteers were simply told to do whatever cleaning and home maintenance the paid social worker deemed necessary. The programme was plagued with a high turnover rate, as volunteers often found the work more unpleasant than they had expected.

In terms of our four criteria, the volunteers did have ownership - they had clients who were their own and no-one else's. But they had little control over what they did as the social worker limited them to a certain list of tasks. There was no clear end result they could see and they were measured only by whether they completed their assigned activities.

In redesigning the job, the staff member responsible for supervision and the volunteer coordinator sat down with a group of volunteers to define results and measures. At this day-long meeting, two desired outcomes were identified. The first was that clients would be able to stay in their homes so long as they had no serious medical problems that made institutionalisation necessary. This result was easily measured by the number of non-medical institutionalisations. Such a result didn't seem enough for the volunteers involved since they felt this could be easily achieved and that they could still be doing a lacklustre job. They suggested that a second outcome be included, that client houses be clean. This raised the problem of how to measure whether a house was clean, since people have different standards of acceptable cleanliness. After much discussion, the group finally decided that the client should be the one to determine if the house was clean or not. The final statement of this second result was *'Clients will be satisfied with the cleanliness of their homes.'*

Determining how to measure this second outcome raised two key questions: *'What information will tell us that we are doing a good job?'* and *'How will we collect it?'* As in most cases, the answer was implied by the desired outcome statement itself. The information required was the opinion of the client. Volunteers could get this information informally by asking the client at the end of their visit whether they were

(continued overleaf)

satisfied. The programme also solicited the opinions of clients on a more formal basis, through a monthly survey. The results of this survey, in terms of numbers of satisfied clients, was then fed back to the volunteers.

Within the framework of what would be deemed acceptable results, the volunteer was then given the authority to do the thinking necessary to achieve them. Instead of the social worker figuring out what needed to be done, the volunteer was given the responsibility to work this out with the client. Success in fulfilling this responsibility was measured by the degree to which the two results were achieved. Where volunteers were having difficulty achieving client satisfaction, they naturally turned to their supervisor for help and advice, as to what they should do differently.

This change in the way the job was defined had a transforming effect on all concerned. The social worker was relieved of the enormous burden of determining what chores needed to be done for each client, and could concentrate on actually doing social work. This made the social worker happier and, because she was able to work personally with isolated clients, it also resulted in a reduction in the number of clients who complained – because complaining was the only way they knew how – to cope with their loneliness.

The volunteers got greater satisfaction from their work, as they were responsible not just for doing odious chores but for keeping their clients out of a nursing home – a much more rewarding role. They had the authority to devise ways of achieving this and they had clear measures of whether they were achieving their results. As a consequence, volunteer turnover was greatly reduced, dropping to a negligible level, and the volunteer programme developed a statewide reputation for good client service.

In this scenario, the volunteer director's role also changed. Instead of assigning volunteers to clients and then trying desperately to keep them interested in doing the task (by organising recognition dinners, providing certificates of appreciation, giving motivational talks, and other highly time-consuming measures), s/he was now a resource person volunteers sought out whenever they perceived they weren't achieving their results. Recruiting time was greatly reduced due to a much lower volunteer turnover. And the amount of time spent in 'motivating' volunteers also dropped, since the job itself had become more rewarding.

CASE STUDY (CONT)
Here is an excerpt from the final job description:

Title:
Senior Service Aide

Purpose:
Clients will be satisfied with the tidiness and cleanliness of their homes.

Suggested Activities:
- Identify tasks clients can't do themselves and want done.
- Recommend tasks clients cannot do to the supervisor for approval.
- Devise ways clients can do more for themselves.
- Complete approved household chores.

Measures:
- Client response on periodic survey.
- Number of client compliments and complaints.

Qualifications:
Skills in listening and the ability to communicate well with diverse populations is essential. Ability to use common household cleaning apparatus such as vacuums and sponge mops is desirable.

Time frame:
Must be able to devote four hours per week for a minimum of two months. Scheduling will be made to meet the availability of the volunteer as long as it is convenient for the client.

Site:
Volunteers will work in the homes of their individual clients.

Supervision:
Volunteers will report to the Senior Service supervisor in their area. Their daily work will not be closely supervised.

Benefits:
Volunteers will receive training in elements of gerontology and in household cleaning as needed. While on the job, volunteers will have full liability insurance. Mileage will be reimbursed at a rate of XXX per mile. Other out-of pocket expenses will also be reimbursed. A work record will be kept for each volunteer so that the position will provide them with good job references. Regular social events such as pot-lucks are held for volunteers at which they are recognised for their valuable contributions.

NEGOTIATING AND UPDATING

While the job descriptions should be formally constructed before recruiting volunteers, it should not be considered an immutable, finished document. Volunteer programmes only succeed when volunteers are motivated to do the job. To ensure this, the job description needs to adapt to meet the needs of the volunteer.

As the interviewer attempts to match the job to the needs and interests of potential volunteers, some negotiation may take place. Further negotiation should take place after the volunteer has been accepted and has begun work. As the volunteer gains more familiarity with the actual work to be done, s/he may make suggestions as to how the job might be modified to make it even more rewarding.

As Ivan Scheier pointed out fifteen years ago, this is in some sense the opposite of what we do with paid staff. There we expect the person to accommodate him or herself to the job. With volunteers, we need to accommodate the job to the individual. We need to build jobs volunteers want to do.

A second circle *(left)* can then be added to the circle of staff needs discussed at the beginning of this chapter. This is the circle of what volunteers want to do. Where there is overlap between the circles, where volunteers are doing things they want to do and that staff want done, we have the building blocks of a strong volunteer programme.

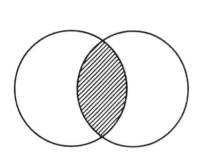

These circles represent the overlap between the needs of the organisation and the motivational needs of the volunteer. The area where the two circles overlap represents the volunteer job which will both benefit the organisation and be suitable for the individual volunteer.

CHAPTER FOUR

RECRUITMENT

MEETING THE NEEDS OF POTENTIAL VOLUNTEERS

Recruitment of volunteers can be difficult, because there is no monetary benefit in undertaking the task. However, if you recruit the right volunteer for the job, they will provide your organisation not only with an extra resource but also with motivated, committed advocates. This chapter details the stages of recruiting the right volunteer - not only for your organisation but also for their own personal benefit.

Recruitment is the process of enlisting volunteers into the work of the organisation. Because volunteers only volunteer their time if they are motivated to do so, recruitment is not a process of persuading a person into an activity they didn't think they wanted to do. Rather, recruitment should be seen as the process of showing people they can do something they already want to do.

In recruiting volunteers, you want to find people who are attracted by the challenge of the job and achieving the results outlined in the volunteer job description. You might picture the process of matching two sets of needs – those of the volunteer and those of the organisation. In Chapter Three, you saw how good volunteer jobs are created by identifying the needs and aspirations of staff. Now you will construct a *circle of volunteer needs*, representing those things which a volunteer might want from an organisation, including such items as interesting work, flexibility, or recognition.

The recruitment process then becomes an effort to identify and reach those volunteers whose circles of needs are congruent with

Topics covered include:

◆ **Meeting the needs of the volunteer**

◆ **Recruiting methods**

◆ **Recruiting in difficult areas**

◆ **Recruiting groups of volunteers**

◆ **Overcoming volunteer's concerns**

◆ **Identifying the positive aspects of the job**

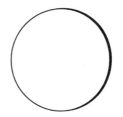

This circle can be constructed for each individual volunteer, because each will have a slightly different mix of needs and motivations.

what the organisation needs and wants, i.e., whose motivational needs can be met by the volunteer position which the organisation has to offer. It is essential to remember that the recruitment process begins, and in many ways hinges upon, the creation of a good volunteer job. If you ask a person *'What would it take to get you to volunteer some of your time for this organisation?'* the answers you get tend not to be about the recruitment technique but about the type of job you are offering. Nearly all will say something like *'It would have to be an interesting job,'* or *'It would have to be something that I felt was worthwhile,'* or *'It should be work that allowed me to grow'*. Attempting to recruit without first having developed worthwhile jobs to offer potential volunteers is equivalent to attempting to sell a product to people who have no need for it. It can be done, but the buyer may well become unhappy later. And when volunteers are unhappy, they don't stay around long.

The recruitment process might also be pictured as a 'funnel'. It is the procedure of identifying and separating from the entire universe of potential volunteers (the whole population of your community) those persons who best might fit the needs of the organisation and its work, and of separating out those who do not.

Organisations recruiting volunteers may suffer from two very different types of recruitment problems. One problem, which is universally feared by new volunteer managers, is that of not having enough volunteers. The second problem, which is much more subtle and yet much more common, is of not having enough of the 'right' volunteers, and, indeed, of usually having too many of the 'wrong' ones.

Effective recruitment consists of attracting just enough of the right volunteers. This distinction is an important one, with significant implications for a volunteer manager. Inexperienced volunteer managers often think that it is desirable to have large numbers of potential volunteers seeking work with the organisation. Unfortunately, in practice a surplus of volunteers can cause difficulties. If you advertise for volunteers for a position, and have only room for two volunteers, what do you do if twenty show up? Initially, you must expend significant amounts of time in the screening and interviewing process, determining which of the volunteers should be accepted. Then you must 'reject' most of the volunteers, risking the prospect of their becoming resentful. The only thing worse than having to reject these volunteers is accepting their service when you don't really have work for them to do, at which point they will really become convinced that both you and the organisation are incompetent.

Recruitment, then, becomes a matter of proportion, balancing the need for applicants with the work required and separating the qualified from the unqualified.

> " Effective recruitment consists of attracting just enough of the right volunteers "

HOW TO RECRUIT VOLUNTEERS

❶ WARM BODY RECRUITMENT

Warm body recruitment is effective when you are trying to recruit for a volunteer position that can be done by most people, either because no special skills are required or because almost anyone can be taught the necessary skills in a limited amount of time. Examples of volunteer jobs suitable for warm body recruitment include a 'hugger' at a Special Olympics event or a worker in an information booth. Warm body recruitment is particularly effective when seeking large numbers of volunteers for simple short-term jobs, like those who would help at a special event, like a festival or a fun run.

Methods for warm body recruitment

Warm body recruitment consists of spreading the message about the potential volunteer position to as broad an audience as possible. The theory is that somewhere among this audience will be enough people who find this position interesting.

The primary methods for warm body recruitment are:

◆ Distribution of organisation brochures or posters advertising the need for volunteers.

◆ Use of public service announcements on television or radio, or newspaper advertisements or publicity.

◆ Contacting community groups such as a neighbourhood association or the Scouts which can provide the person power.

Distribution of organisation brochures

There are a great number of possible sites for distribution of printed information. The aim is to place brochures in locations where people are likely to pick them up and read them, and or where people can actually use the brochures to advise the people who seek their advice. Possible sites include:

◆ Job shops and employment centres

◆ Libraries

◆ Tourist Information Centres

◆ Chambers of Commerce

◆ Schools and youth clubs

HOW TO RECRUIT VOLUNTEERS

There are three different types of volunteer recruitment processes that can be used.:

❶ WARM BODY RECRUITMENT

❷ TARGETED RECRUITMENT

❸ CONCENTRIC CIRCLE RECRUITMENT

Each is quite different in what it seeks to accomplish and in what it is effective in accomplishing.

◆ Church bulletin boards
◆ Community centres
◆ Volunteer Bureaux
◆ Hospital waiting rooms and clinics
◆ Shop window information boards

Those volunteer programmes which deliver a service within an identifiable neighbourhood might best benefit from a simple 'door-to-door' distribution campaign.

Public service announcements

With an ad on television or radio, or a good classified ad in the local newspaper, perhaps only .01% of the audience will be interested. But if over one million people see the ad this could result in 100 applicants.

Despite the efforts to involve volunteers through the mass media, it is difficult to rely on this method to solve all of your recruitment problems. A 1990 Gallup Poll in the US showed only 6% of all volunteers reported finding out about their volunteer job via mass media.

Volunteer Classified Ads

The King County Sexual Assault Centre

believes that all people, including children, have the right to be free to live without the fear of sexual violence. You also believe that victims of sexual abuse and their non-offending family members deserve support to alleviate the trauma of sexual abuse in their lives. Volunteer opportunities are currently available in a variety of areas and we are recruiting now for our October and January training sessions. Please call xxx to help eliminate sexual violence in your community.

Death Valley National Monument
- This large desert valley,

nearly surrounded by high mountains, contains the lowest point in the Western Hemisphere and is known as the hottest spot in North America. Here you can find spectacular wild flower displays, sand dunes, Scotty's Castle, and remnants of the gold and borax mining days. Volunteer Jobs: Opportunities that exist in the winter are involved with interpretation, camp ground host programme, and curatorial work. Contact: Death Valley National Monument, xxx

It may be difficult to describe a complicated job in the short framework of a newspaper ad or a radio or television public service announcement. If you do attempt to construct such an ad, you might wish to concentrate on 'selling' the needs of your client population, since it will be simpler to describe their needs than it will be to describe the entire job. Other needs which can usefully be mentioned include the provision of training or other support to the volunteer in preparing for the job, and the availability of flexible scheduling to make it easier for the volunteer to meet the time requirements for the job.

The following are some sample newspaper classified ads which are both brief and sufficiently compelling:

Volunteer Classified Ads

It is important to realise that even if ads like the above do attract a volunteer, they will not by themselves guarantee that recruitment is successful. You will still need to motivate the potential volunteer about the job and the work of the organisation. The mass media techniques will simply serve to get you close enough to the volunteer to make an actual recruitment pitch.

Speaking to community groups

One of the best methods for warm body recruitment is to arrange presentations to local clubs and other groups. Such presentations can serve both to inform the public about what your organisation does and to recruit new volunteers. In following this method of recruitment, be sure to:

◆ Deliberately select those groups you wish to speak to. There are two types who are most helpful: groups whose membership regularly participates in helping out in the community (Rotary, service clubs, etc.), and groups whose membership as individuals are likely to have a common interest with your cause. Schedule these types of groups first.

◆ In seeking an opportunity to speak to the group, consider going through a group member. Members can serve as your authenticators to their peer group, paving your way to a more receptive audience with the person responsible for making the decision. They can also make it more likely that you will be invited to speak. Many groups have a social secretary who is desperate to find good speakers.

◆ Try to time your speaking to meet both the group's and your needs. Find out about other projects the group is already committed to, and time your talk to coincide with their need to develop a new project. Determine how much lead time they need and make sure that your request is not too immediate for them to be able to meet.

◆ Pick your presenters carefully. Make sure the person who is speaking can explain what your organisation does and exactly what is needed from the volunteers. Consider sending a volunteer who can speak forcefully about the worth of the volunteer job.

◆ If possible, use a visual presentation (slides, pictures, etc.) to increase interest. If your presentation is boring, the group may assume that your jobs will be too.

◆ Be prepared for people to offer their services. Take along brochures, examples of jobs for which they are needed, sign-up sheets, etc. If someone expresses interest, don't leave without their name and phone number, and commit yourself to following up their interest. Follow up as quickly as possible.

♦ Be prepared for too much success. You may need to have a backup plan to handle the entire group wanting to volunteer together to help you, and not just a few individuals. If several group members decide to volunteer, you might want to consider ways in which they might work together as a group while performing the volunteer work.

♦ Remember that at some point during your presentation you should directly and unequivocally **ask** the audience to volunteer. Very few people will insist on volunteering for your programme without being asked to do so.

❷ TARGETED RECRUITMENT

The second method for volunteer recruitment is called targeted recruitment. With this approach you determine the kind of person who would really like to do the job and track them down. Start by examining the motivations and backgrounds of current volunteers in the position to find out if there are any common factors. Do they all have the same type of motivation? Do they have similar backgrounds or education or experiences or occupations? Do they come from similar groups? Did they all hear about the job in the same fashion? Common factors will enable you to identify populations which seem to like the job despite its requirements, and the commonality will enable you to locate others from that population group. But remember that who you have may be determined by how you have recruited in the past.

Recent research studies can provide examples of this approach. A study of 4-H (a US volunteer program with young people as clients) volunteer leaders found that 4-H volunteers who continued in their leadership roles tended to differ from their discontinuing counterparts in geographical location, number of children in the family and number of children who had participated in 4-H. Other studies have found that individuals willing to work as volunteers in the field of mental retardation differed from non-volunteers in that they placed less emphasis on success (both social and economic) and greater emphasis on values such as equality, personal expression, and growth.

A targeted recruitment campaign involves answering a series of questions:

I   What is the job that needs to be done?

As stressed already, it is the job, and the opportunity to do something that meets the volunteer's motivational needs, that is the key to attracting most volunteers. A general message, such as

'Volunteers are needed at the Crisis Clinic' , doesn't let anyone know what the volunteers do there. As such, the message doesn't indicate to a potential volunteer that there is anything which they might find interesting.

Volunteer managers who send such a general message tend to do so for one or two reasons. The first is that it is so obvious to everyone in the organisation what the volunteers do that they assume the entire community is familiar with their efforts as well, such as with the Samaritans. If the organisation does a good job of community education, this may well be so, but not all potentially interested volunteers may have got the message.

The second reason volunteer managers send general messages is that there are so many things volunteers do at the organisation. As you will see in the next few sections effective recruitment must be targeted to particular segments of the population. Different jobs in an organisation will appeal to different people with particular motivational needs. By targeting the campaign at different groups, you can stress specific jobs that appeal to those groups and avoid the flabbiness of a message that mentions no attractive jobs.

II Who would want to do the job that needs to be done?

This is a question that most of us don't bother to ask, because you have been able to recruit successful volunteers from a variety of backgrounds. It is easier to recruit the right person for the job if you have answered this question, because it is easier to target your message to the needs of that particular group. Messages sent to the community in general have to apply to everyone and often wind up speaking to no one in particular.

Ask yourself if there is a certain type of person who is being sought. Do you want someone from a specific age group? Do you want someone of a particular sex or ethnic background? Do you want someone with certain professional skills? The answers to these questions may be multiple – you may want young, old, and middle-aged people, for example. But if you have reached this conclusion in a thoughtful way (rather than merely saying, *'We'll take any age group.'*), you can then begin to target a recruitment campaign on each of these groups, with a slightly different message to each.

The advantage of sending a slightly different message to each group is that you have a better chance of speaking directly to that group's motivational needs. You will therefore tend to get a larger percentage of people from each group to consider volunteering for your organisation than you otherwise would. For example, if you identify newcomers to town as a potential group of volunteers, you might stress jobs in which they can meet new people, and your volunteer recruiting efforts would spotlight efforts in which people work as teams. If you identify harried executives as potential volunteers, on the other hand, you might stress jobs that can be done conveniently within a busy or unpredictable schedule, even at home, and which have a fixed end point.

By examining and interviewing your current volunteer population, you should get a good start in developing a list of targets. But you should be careful not to assume that this list will represent **all** of the potential groups who might be interested in the job. Once you have developed a list of the characteristics of the volunteers who have enjoyed the job, start thinking about what other types of people are likely to have similar backgrounds or interests, and try to expand the list of potential targets before you begin analysing how to locate and approach each potential target group.

Targeted recruitment tends to work best when you are looking for a particular type of skill, such as experience in accounting. It tends to work somewhat with psychological characteristics, but only if they are sufficiently identifiable (such as a love for children or a liking for sports) that they can be readily recognised by going beyond internal mental states into outward physical manifestations.

III Where will you find them?

Once you have determined who you are trying to recruit, you can ask 'Where will you find them?' If you are after a certain type of profession, are there professional societies or clubs where such people might be found? If you are after members of a given age group

One of the most difficult notions to accept about targeted recruitment is that somewhere in this world there are people who will want to do what will seem to you to be the strangest volunteer jobs, ones that you cannot imagine anyone actually *wanting* to do. An article in the *Wall Street Journal* commenting on a group of volunteer professionals in New York City notes:

The wide variety of chores is an advantage. Volunteers stand ready to give time, but are not sure what jobs they can handle. One young woman, for instance, explained that she started taking city children on outings but discovered 'I couldn't stand kids.' Now she hauls trash from housing-rehab sites. 'You'd be surprised,' she says, 'at the satisfaction you can get when you see a dumpster finally fill up.'

Not your typical volunteer job, perhaps, but one that is quite satisfying to some people whose regular work doesn't give them that sense of definitive accomplishment.

or a certain ethnic group, are there places where groups of such people gather? Where do they shop? Where do they worship? Where do they go for recreational activity? Again, if you simply begin trying to recruit anyone in the general community, the answer to this questions is 'everywhere.' This answer makes your job that much more difficult because it will be harder to focus your recruitment effort. People who are everywhere are also nowhere in particular.

The answer to the question *Where will you find them?'* has a lot to do with the recruitment methods that can be used. For example, if you are trying to recruit 'Yuppies' you might see

---

PROMPT QUESTIONS

'WHO WOULD WANT TO DO THIS JOB?'

1 Who currently does it?

What jobs or occupations do they have?

2 Who once did it and has now left or retired?

3 Who would like to be doing it, but is now in a job where it is not possible? Who was educated to do this, but now has a different type of job?

4 Who could learn to do it?

5 Who is now learning to do it and intends to do it more in the future? What schools or colleges teach this subject?

6 Who can get someone else who is qualified to do it? Can you find a teacher or a senior practitioner in this skill who can recommend & encourage others in their field to help you?

7 Who has a radically different job, such that this would be an exciting novelty?

---

about putting advertisements on grocery bags in up-market supermarkets or put flyers on the windscreens of BMWs. If you are recruiting teenagers with time on their hands, you might distribute leaflets outside school or give a talk to the sixth form. Several volunteer programmes have recruited single people by advertising in singles bars. If potential volunteers live in a particular neighbourhood, you might go door-to-door (a technique often used by neighbourhood and community associations).

The answer might also lead us to speak to certain groups. Such groups might be formal or informal, and your talk to them might be a prepared speech or a casual conversation. Communities tend to be made up of circles of people – social groups, groups of employees, clubs, professional organisations, etc. In identifying who you are after and where they are to be found, you will move towards identifying the circles of people you want to reach in order to present your recruitment message.

People also belong to readership, listening, and viewing groups. If you are going to use the media in your campaign, you need to select which media to use based on the profile of its listeners/ viewers/readers. Any newspaper, radio station, or television station can supply you with such information.

IV How should you go about communicating with them?

As indicated above, once you have listed some locations where people can be found, the fourth step is to ask *'How will you communicate your recruiting message to them?'* This step is implied by the previous one, and if you have done a good job of figuring out where they can be reached, developing an appropriate message is easy.

In general, the most effective methods of recruiting a volunteer are those in which two-way communication is possible. The best form is through a current volunteer or board member, since they are attributed with purer motives than those of paid staff. There is always the possible subconscious suspicion that the paid person is trying to get the potential volunteer to do some of the work that the staff member does not want to do.

One of the weaknesses of having no particular target group in mind is that it is difficult to use methods that involve two-way communication with the general populace. If you are trying to recruit 'members of the general community' who are 'everywhere' you have to fall back on one-way communication such as direct mail, press releases, posters, public service announcements, grocery bag messages, newspaper ads, handbills or phone-in calls. Such efforts do succeed in recruiting volunteers, but they are less efficient in recruiting effective, dedicated volunteers than those methods in which a potential volunteer can ask questions and where you can directly address the candidate's own needs and skills.

People volunteer only because they want to. Helping a person see that they can do something that they want to do is easiest when a two-way conversation can take place. Therefore, while you should include easy and inexpensive methods of recruiting volunteers in any recruitment drive, you will be most effective if you put an emphasis on one-to-one conversations and on talking to groups small enough to get a good two-way conversation going.

Recruiting through such methods is a more labour-intensive way of going about it than a one-way communication campaign. Again, this means involving other people in the recruitment process. It means the volunteer coordinator needs to manage the recruiting effort, not do it all themselves.

V What are the motivational needs of these people?

It is important that the recruitment message speaks directly to the motivational needs of the potential volunteer. It must appeal to the reason the volunteer wants to do the job. If, for example, you are going to target newcomers to town in your recruitment campaign, you might surmise that one of their motivational needs would be to make new friends. You would then make sure that your recruitment campaign includes the information that the volunteer would meet lots of friendly, interesting people while doing the valuable work you are asking of them.

In addition to doing something worthwhile, each individual has a complex of other motivations for volunteering. When you identify your target groups, you can then guess at which needs might be most important to individuals in that group. You can then send a message which speaks directly to those needs. People might respond to messages stressing motivators as diverse as patriotism, a need to protect their families, or a need to advance their careers. On the right, for example, is a very effective ad designed to recruit macho males.

This speaks effectively to a person who has a need to feel he is tough, and who has a need to test himself against very demanding physical circumstances. It was used by Scott and Shackelton for their Antarctic expedition. A similar appeal was used successfully by a volunteer director who had been having a very difficult time trying to find people to escort children to school through gang-infested housing projects.

POSSIBLE MOTIVES FOR VOLUNTEERING

- ◆ To 'get out of the house'
- ◆ To get to know important people in the community
- ◆ To establish a 'track record' to help get a job and gain new skills
- ◆ To make a transition from prison, mental illness or other situations to the 'real world'
- ◆ To 'test the waters' before making a career change
- ◆ To make new friends
- ◆ To be with old friends who are already volunteering in the organisation
- ◆ To gain knowledge about the problems of the community
- ◆ To maintain skills no longer used
- ◆ To impress present employer
- ◆ To spend 'quality time' with members of their family by volunteering together
- ◆ To gain status
- ◆ To escape boredom
- ◆ To feel part of a group
- ◆ To express a religious or philosophical belief
- ◆ To exercise skills in a different context

MEN WANTED for hazardous journey

Small wages, bitter cold, long months of complete darkness, constant danger, safe return doubtful. Honour and recognition in case of success.

VI **What will you say to them?**

The sixth major step is to develop an effective recruitment message. Often no thought is given to this at all – you just send people out to talk about what the organisation does and about the kinds of volunteer jobs you want people to do. By doing this, you needlessly reduce the number of people who will respond to you.

An effective recruiting message has four parts, the first of which is *a statement of the need*. The statement of need tells the volunteer why the job s/he will be doing is important. Most recruiting messages seldom talk about why you want the person to do a particular job. They only talk about the activities the person will be performing. This leaves it up to the person being recruited to figure out what the need for those activities is.

The need

The need usually refers to something that exists in the community, not something that exists inside the organisation. *'Our OAP centre needs volunteers to help cook hot meals for pensioners one day a week'* is not the kind of statement you are referring to. The problem with such a statement is that it conjures up only the picture of sweating over a hot stove, and there are few people who are likely to be excited about doing that. Many, however, would find their interest engaged by the opportunity to do something to enhance the lives of the elderly. By including such a statement of need in the recruitment message, you show people how they can help solve a problem rather than merely undertake an activity.

Statements of need naturally lead the potential volunteer to think *'That's terrible; somebody should do something about that.'* Once the person is thinking this way, it is a simple step to recognising that they could be that person. Recruiting them then becomes easy.

THE NEED

Often, for volunteers involved in providing a direct service, the need will be that of the clients to be served. A few such statements of needs are listed in an abbreviated form below:

◆ **Hospital Volunteer:** *'Many long stay patients in the hospital are lonely and depressed.'*

◆ **Crisis Clinic Volunteer:** *'Some people in our community suffer from mental fear and anguish so intense that they do harm to themselves and to other people.'*

◆ **Literacy Volunteer:** *'Many people from all walks of life are unable to take advantage of the full benefits or our society because they are unable to read or write.'*

◆ **Girl Scout Leader:** *'Many girls grow up without the self-confidence and other skills to become competent, successful adults.'*

◆ **Mental Health Receptionist:** *'Clients coming into the centre are often embarrassed, confused, and uneasy.'*

◆ **Museum Guide:** *'Many people who will visit the museum would like to know more about the exhibits. Sometimes their lack of knowledge causes them to miss a great deal of the meaning and beauty of the exhibits, and their interest in returning to the museum wanes.'*

◆ **Neighbourhood Visitor:** *'Some pensioners live in housing developments with little or no contact with other people or the outside world. They are sometimes sick, in need of assistance, or in some instances, dying, and no one is aware of their plight.'*

In responding to statements of need, the volunteer is directly answering the needs that the organisation itself exists to address. On the other hand, some volunteers are recruited to do things that do not directly affect the organisation's main work. Some clerical types of volunteer jobs, for example, exist to meet the needs of staff or of the organisation more than they do the needs of clients or the community.

PEOPLE ARE HUNGRY

Somebody should do something about that.

BE SOMEBODY.
Call [the organisation].

A very powerful and simple recruitment message

In talking about the need in such circumstances, it is important to talk about the needs of the staff in the context of their work in meeting the needs of the community. A few examples are listed below:

♦ **Voluntary Action Centre Clerk/Typist:** *'When people call up wondering what they can do to help make the community a better place, staff are sometimes limited in their responses because the information is not filed systematically and not typed.'*

♦ **Community Organisation Bookkeeper:** *'In order to continue our efforts to improve the lives of the poor, you must account for our grants properly, a skill none of our staff have.'*

The statement of need should lead the potential volunteer naturally to the conclusion that something ought to be done about it. In one-to-one or small group situations, the recruiter can stop at this point to check to see if the potential volunteers agree that this is a need worth doing something about. Often, in such situations, the potential volunteer may stop to remark on the seriousness of the situation. Once you get a volunteer thinking that somebody should do something about the problem, recruitment is as easy as showing them that they could be that somebody.

Returning to our example of the old people's centre, the recruiter might ask the potential volunteer if s/he was aware that many senior citizens in the community were unable to afford nutritionally balanced meals and were suffering from malnutrition. The recruitee might include some anecdotal evidence or some statistics, though these are often less compelling in conversation than stories or case studies about actual people. If the volunteer doesn't say anything, the recruiter might ask what s/he thinks about it.

The job

All this then leads naturally to the second element of an effective recruitment message, which is to show the volunteer how he or she can help solve this problem. In other words, now is the time to talk about the job description or what you want the volunteer to do. By describing these activities in the context of the need, you make your recruitment message more powerful. If you merely jump in and talk about the activities without also defining the need, some people will be able to figure out why such activities are important, but others won't. By making the assumption that people will automatically see why the work is worth doing, you needlessly screen out people who would like to give their time to a worthwhile effort, but aren't able to see immediately why this job is important. Using our example, the potential volunteer might be quite eager to help out in the kitchen to help overcome the problem of malnutrition, while s/he may be totally uninterested in the job if it is merely described as cooking, washing dishes, or serving meals.

> **In the old people's centre, the potential volunteer might be quite eager to help out in the kitchen to help overcome the problem of malnutrition, while s/he may be totally uninterested in the job if it is merely described as cooking, washing dishes, or serving meals.**

When talking to a potential volunteer about a job, the recruiter should attempt to help the volunteer see themselves doing the job. People only do what they can picture themselves doing, so you need to make your description of the job as vivid as possible. Talk about the physical environment, the people they will meet, and all the minor details that create a full image of the situation the volunteer will encounter.

> The questions should assume that the person is indeed going to volunteer. Avoid saying 'If you decide to do this.' Instead, ask questions such as:
>
> ◆ **'What hours will be best for you?'**
>
> ◆ **'What appeals to you most about this work?'**
>
> ◆ **'What can we do to make the experience fun for you?'**
>
> ◆ **'Will you be able to attend our staff meetings?'**

The picture you create should stress the positive elements of the job in order to encourage the person to volunteer, but you should also be honest. Although recruiting does have something in common with selling a product, you must refuse to glamorise or misrepresent the job. If you are trying to sell the volunteer a new truck, you might exaggerate the positive aspects of the vehicle, but in recruiting you are trying to show them that s/he can do something they really want to do. If s/he volunteers under a false impression, you will only waste a lot of time in training and trying to motivate a person who probably will not last long in the job.

In addition to painting a picture of the job to be done, you need to put the volunteer in the picture. The recruiter should always talk about what 'you' will be doing, not about what 'a volunteer' will do. A good technique to use in this regard is to ask the person some questions about how s/he would react in certain job situations. These situations should be easy and pleasant ones to handle, not questions such as *'What will you do if a client throws up on you'?*

Fears

For some situations, it will be desirable to address potential fears that a volunteer might have about the job.

The best way to deal with the issues is to be straightforward, letting the volunteer know that the organisation recognises the problem and then letting the volunteer know what steps the organisation has already taken to help counter the problem. Steps could include, for example, providing extensive training for the volunteer, conducting an orientation in how to protect oneself against infection, or providing regular health checks, etc.

Most volunteers are more afraid of the unknown than of any recognised risk. This means that potential problems are less likely to deter them from volunteering if they are addressed openly, and if the organisation seems to be responsible in dealing with them.

Often the easiest way to address these fears is during a one-to-one discussion with a volunteer, but they can also be addressed in other formats, as the newspaper advertisement *(right)* shows. The advertisment addresses two potential fears. The first is a lack of qualification for the task of counselling, which is rebutted in the sentence that follows offering 'extensive training.' The other fear is that the job is only being offered to 'professionals', which is countered in the next to last sentence.

Fears might include such things as:

◆ A clientele that is viewed as dangerous

◆ A type of work at which the volunteer has little experience

◆ A part of town that is unfamiliar to the volunteer

◆ A disease that is viewed as potentially dangerous or infectious to the volunteer

---

VOLUNTEER COUNSELLORS NEEDED

The Fairfax Victim Assistance Network is accepting applications from volunteers to join a dedicated team who counsel victims of domestic violence and sexual assault.

Extensive training will be provided in March on counselling skills, crisis intervention, advocacy and community resources.

Persons with diverse backgrounds and life experiences are encouraged to apply.

Call xxx-xxxx for info and an application form.

Benefits

In addition to talking about the need and the job, the message should also talk about how the experience will allow the volunteer to meet the motivational needs required from the job. This fourth part of the message, the benefits, helps people see how they can help themselves by doing activities that help the organisation serve the community.

To be as effective as possible, the recruitment message needs to show the potential volunteer that whatever combination of need s/he has can be met by the organisation. This section of the message is particularly important in recruiting volunteers for clerical or staff support jobs, such as the legendary envelope stuffer. People don't volunteer to stuff envelopes because of the job or for the satisfaction of creating mountains of mail. They do it for some other reason, the most common being the pleasure of socialising with a group of other people while they do this important but not very exciting task.

> **A person who wants to help in an old people's centre might have a hobby of photography. As the recruiter talks about helping out in the kitchen (which is what the organisation wants the volunteer to do), s/he may notice that the volunteer is only mildly interested in that particular job. When talking about photography, however, their interest perks up. S/he might then ask if the volunteer would be interested in using the recruitees photographic skills to help the centre.**

If the recruitment message is presented in a one-way format, it should list some of the benefits that the volunteer coordinator thinks will appeal to the target group. If it is being presented in a two-way format, where the recruiter has an opportunity to talk to potential volunteers about their needs, skills, and desires, the benefits can be tailored specifically to the audience.

Because each volunteer has a different combination of motivations for volunteering, the recruiter needs to know something about the potential volunteers in order to do the most effective job of encouraging them to volunteer. If people want to gain job experience, for example, you should propose jobs that allow them to do that.

If the recruiter doesn't know the person s/he is trying to recruit, and if the circumstances allow, s/he should spend some time with the person to find out what kinds of benefits might appeal. This situation also provides the opportunity to identify some things the potential volunteer is concerned about and enjoys doing, and other clues to what it is s/he wants to do. This may lead to the development of new volunteer opportunities.

If the recruiter learns what kinds of benefits are important to the volunteer, it is important that these be communicated to the volunteer coordinator so that s/he can make sure the volunteer's needs are met. One cause of volunteer turnover is that volunteers don't get the things they volunteered to get. They volunteered to be with particular friends and got assigned to different shifts; they volunteered to get involved in a regular, soothing, non-stressful activity and were given a high-risk task; they volunteered to learn new skills and never got the chance to do anything beyond what they already knew; they volunteered to impress their employer and never got a letter of thanks sent to their boss; and so on. The information obtained from effective recruiting is the same information that can be used in successful volunteer retention.

The statement of benefits in the recruitment message, like the statement of need, is often omitted by recruiters – perhaps because they ascribe purer motives to volunteers or because it is so obvious to them. Leaving this out, however, needlessly reduces the number of people you can attract to assist your organisation.

Stating *the need*, the *job*, the negating of *fears*, and *stressing the benefits* are all essential if you are to have the best chance of recruiting as many effective people as possible. Regardless of the types of recruitment methods you use, tell the people what the problem is *(show the need)*; show them how they can help solve it *(describe the job)*; alleviate their concerns *(deal with fears)*; and tell them what they will gain *(indicate the benefits)* in the process.

CHILDREN ARE BEING ABUSED

You can help them by offering tempory shelter.

We'll show you how you can help these children and help yourself at the same time.

Call (phone number)

Even if the space is limited, include all these elements in your message. Here, for example, is a four sentence recruitment message that fits on a poster

VII Who will do it?

The seventh step in preparing an effective targeted recruitment campaign is to consider *'Who will do the recruiting?'* This is where you decide how to bring more two-way communication into the recruiting effort and who will take the responsibility for creating posters, contacting radio stations, and other forms of one-way communication.

An often overlooked and extremely effective resource is a person who is recruited specifically to recruit other volunteers. If you are looking for volunteers from the workplace, for example, an effective first step is to recruit an employee whose volunteer job is to identify other potential volunteers within the company and recruit them for jobs that they would want to do. Such a person can play this role year-round, thus providing more flexibility than other means of recruitment. Every time a need for a volunteer arises, the volunteer coordinator can put the word out through the volunteer recruiters. These people can then approach people they know who might be interested in the new opportunity to volunteer.

An effective volunteer programme might have volunteer recruiters in a variety of different groups in the community at large. Such a network, once established, enables the volunteer coordinator to use the most effective form of recruitment – face-to-face contact with someone you know – in a systematic and easy way. A good way of setting up such a system is to have staff, committee members, and other volunteers think about people they know in the various community groups who might be willing to volunteer their time in this way. These people can then be brought together for a training session.

> 66
>
> **The most effective people to be involved in recruitment are often those who are volunteers or management committee members of the organisation. In order to ensure their effectiveness, however, you need to be sure they know that this is their responsibility, who they are supposed to recruit, where to find those people, how they are supposed to do it, and what they are supposed to say. In short, they need to be well prepared by the volunteer coordinator to do the most effective job possible.**
>
> 99

VIII   How will they know what to do?

The last step in preparing the recruitment effort is to train those who will be delivering the recruitment message. If you follow the principles described above, this means training everyone involved with the organisation and its work. Everybody knows potential volunteers; it's just a matter of getting them to think about asking people they know to make a commitment to solving the organisation needs and of equipping them to make a coherent case for doing so.

In general, training should cover the participant's role in the recruitment process and provide adequate opportunity for them to role-play their presentation of the recruitment message. Ways to make sure participants learn from the training experience are covered in the chapter on training.

Combining targeting & warm body recruitment

By carefully wording your mass media communication you can actually make use of targeted recruitment. Consider this elegant ad, *(on the right)* from Washington, DC.

While distributed via mass media, this ad makes use of targeted wording to appeal to a certain audience. The key words 'behind the scenes' provide a strong incentive to those of artistic bent who wish either to meet and mingle with stars or to get to help with stagecraft. Contrast its effect with the following ad *(on the right)* which utilises exactly the same wording, but with a very different result.

By utilising targeted recruitment techniques to identify the motivations of likely volunteers you can design a mass media campaign which will generate a greater number of qualified and interested applicants.

Interested in the arts?
•
Volunteers know what goes on behind the scenes at the Kennedy Centre.
•
Call the Friends of the Kennedy Centre.

My Sister's Place, a shelter for battered women and their children.
Hands-on with hot-line and shelter work
Behind the scenes with committee work.

❸ CONCENTRIC CIRCLE RECRUITMENT

Concentric circle recruitment is the lazy way to ensure you have a flow of replacement volunteers applying to work at your organisation. It works through the simple theory that those people who are already connected to you and your organisation are the best targets for a recruitment campaign.

To utilise the concentric circle theory, first attempt to locate a volunteer for the position by starting with the population groups who are already connected to you and then work outwards. You might capitalise on the fact that most volunteers are recruited by those people who they already know by asking the incumbent in the job to recruit a friend of theirs to replace them. You might look among former clients or your current volunteers for a replacement. This approach will make it more likely to get a positive response, because the group of potential volunteers with whom you will be talking will already be favourably disposed toward your organisation. Similar techniques are used in fund-raising (donor get a donor) and in membership drives, for example for a book club (member get a member). They are simple, effective, and cost effective.

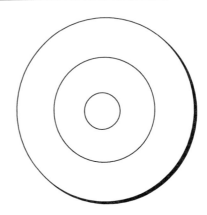

To visualise the theory of concentric circles, simply think of ripples in a pond when a rock is thrown in. Starting in the centre of contact, the ripples spread outwards. Concentric circle volunteer recruitment operates in the same manner.

'WHO ASKED YOU TO VOLUNTEER?'

	%
Friend	52.0
Someone at church or synagogue	28.3
Family member or relative	25.0
My employer	7.9
Organisation representative	7.9
Teacher/school activities leader	4.0
Other	5.1
Don't know	1.8

1990 Gallup Poll - Independent Sector

Ideal groups around whom to structure your concentric circles recruitment include:

◆ Current volunteers

◆ Friends & relatives of volunteers

◆ Clients

◆ Friends & relatives of clients

◆ 'Alumni' (clients & volunteers)

◆ Staff

◆ Donors

◆ People in the neighbourhood

◆ Retirees in your field or subject

These results *(left)* indicate one of the simple reasons for the remarkable success of concentric circle recruitment. Since it often involves face-to-face recruitment by those who already know the people whom they are approaching, one of its strengths is the personal testimony of the asking volunteer. During the conversation, the volunteer can say, either directly or indirectly, *'This is a good volunteer job with a good organisation. I know this because I worked there and I think it is worth your time to work there too.'* This is a very credible and a very persuasive argument that mass media techniques and appeals from complete strangers have a hard time equalling.

Even more direct evidence of the efficacy of concentric circle recruitment was seen in a result of the 1987 Gallup Survey, also available from Independent Sector: among those who have been recipients of services from a community organisation, 23% volunteer; among non-recipients, only 9% volunteer. The service received need not have been given directly by the organisation itself, but may instead be of a similar type to that received by those being asked to volunteer. One campaign to recruit volunteers for the alcoholism treatment unit in a hospital consisted of letters to members of a local Alcoholics Anonymous group. Each letter was jointly signed by the volunteer coordinator of the hospital and by a current member of the AA group (thus tapping two elements of the concentric circle concept).

These examples demonstrate that a clear strength of the concentric circle theory is that it concentrates on approaching those who may already have a good reason for helping out, either because they have received services themselves or they have seen the impact of the services on others. They have thus become convinced both of the need for the services and of the ability of your organisation to assist those with that need; all that remains is to demonstrate to them that *they* are capable of helping in meeting that need.

In short, any population group which has already been favourably exposed to your programme makes an excellent target for a concentric circle recruitment campaign. All you need to do to capitalise on this receptivity is to start a 'word of mouth' recruitment campaign and a constant trickle of potential volunteers will approach your organisation. Continually stress to all of these groups that they are essential to your recruitment campaign, and help them in knowing the types of volunteers for whom you looking and the ways in which they can assist in finding and recruiting these volunteers.

Although a lot of effective person-to-person recruiting 'just happens,' you can make a lot more of it happen by systematically encouraging it. Everyone involved in the organisation, both volunteers and staff, should understand what their recruitment responsibilities are within the framework of the overall plan. Each time a need for a new volunteer arises, the volunteer coordinator should prepare a job description, and a rough statement of the need and possible benefits. This can be communicated to all staff, committee members, and current volunteers (especially those recruited for this purpose) so that they might begin looking, among the people they know, for good candidates.

If you are a new organisation you will probably not be able to take advantage of concentric circle recruitment, and will have to rely on the less effective methods of mass media and targeting. In time, however, you will build up the good will among a sufficient population group to take advantage of this simplest and most efficient method of recruitment.

RECRUITING FOR DIFFICULT SITUATIONS

Recruiting for a 'controversial' cause, for a job perceived as 'dangerous' or for one that is recognised as 'difficult' is obviously harder than for easy jobs. Recruitment can be particularly difficult when the nature of the cause or the job is likely to provoke an initial fear reaction from the potential volunteer. The following are some suggestions for trying to design a recruitment campaign for these types of volunteer positions:

❶ Do advertise via local TV, radio, or newspapers so that thousands of potentially recruitable people see the message. In essence, saturate the community with your recruitment message. Some of the people you reach won't be afraid.

❷ Solicit those who are acquainted with the problem area because they already work with it, or are in an industry related to it, and thus do not have the same level of fear as the general public. Be sure to remember ancillary and connected industries, such as educators who teach in subject areas that discuss the problem area. You can also solicit the families of those who work in the subject area.

❸ Ask those who once worked with the problem or those who are seeking careers related to the cause.

❹ Solicit former clients, their families, and their friends and relatives. This group is less likely to be afraid, more likely to identify with your group because they have received services, and quite likely to be committed to doing something about the problem.

❺ Recruit via current volunteers. Emphasise 'word of mouth' communication. Their personal communication skill (*'I work in this area and I know that it is both safe and rewarding.'*) will often overcome barriers to involvement.

❻ Start with recruiting people for a noncontroversial job in your organisation. Develop a 'two-tier' recruitment system. First recruit them for a safe and easy job, then offer them a tough assignment after they've got to know you better.

❼ Create an educational programme to combat the fear. Start offering seminars in the community offering the true facts about the situation. Utilise some of your more motivated volunteers as spokespeople talking about their experiences. Recruit from those who attend the seminars.

❽ Utilise the targeted recruitment approach, identifying people who would want to do the job. A dangerous job might appeal to certain types of people.

❾ Bring people to you for some completely different reason. The London Lighthouse, for example, organises evening concerts. This gives visitors a chance to come to your premises, perhaps feel warm about your organisation, and pick up a bit of literature.

COMBINING ALTERNATIVE JOB DESIGN WITH RECRUITMENT EFFORTS

It is also possible to enhance your recruitment effort by considering variations in volunteer job design. These variations may be considered where difficulties are encountered in finding adequate numbers of volunteers because of the complexity of the volunteer position under consideration.

Included are:

Gang up on the job

One way to approach difficult recruitment is to make the 'volunteer' not one person, but several. If the difficulty is that the job is too 'large' for a single individual, then the obvious solution is to make it the responsibility of more than one person. You can approach this via two different methods:

Team volunteering

Team volunteering is the classic job-sharing approach to the situation. Make the volunteer unit a partnership, with two persons equally sharing the job, or make the job one done by a 'lead' volunteer who is given an assistant. The team can split up the time and work requirements. This approach is particularly useful when you are attempting to encourage a volunteer who has a particular expertise but is reluctant to volunteer because they don't feel like they have the time necessary to do all of the work. Their volunteer 'aide' can provide the hands; the expert volunteer can provide the brains.

An interesting advantage of team volunteering is that it benefits all parties in the relationship. It will both enable you to induce reluctant volunteers to attempt new challenges and enable you to convince tired volunteers to remain on a bit longer. Another potential advantage of team volunteering is that a properly constructed team may be synergistic, resulting in a whole that is stronger than the sum of its parts. Team members may individually lack skills which are compensated for by other team members, resulting in a more effective work group than any one individual worker can be.

The disadvantages of team volunteering are twofold. First, it requires careful matching of the personalities who will be involved. They must be compatible in personality, vision of the job, and work style to form a team successfully. Second, it requires greater management and supervision, particularly during its early stages when the team is attempting to work out relationships and working arrangements. If you assign volunteers to work together as a team, schedule a review session for about a month after the volunteers have been matched. Turn this session into a discussion

> **Team volunteering can have several advantages as Susan Chambre notes:**
>
> " Teaming up compatible volunteers builds in several key elements that enhance the success of jobs performed by people who work for free: It facilitates recruitment, reduces the need for training, increases the probability of success in performing tasks since one member of the team is more experienced, and addresses the need for sociability. "

of their working relationship, using it to determine whether they have made the transition to a smooth working unit, and using it to determine whether their personalities are suitable for a situation of shared responsibility.

While the word 'team' is used to describe this type of job-sharing relationship, it is important to note that the team should not include more than two people. Job-sharing with three or more people is nearly impossible to accomplish without an extravagant amount of work. Larger groups begin to function more as committees, and the nature of that larger social interaction can result in factions and alliances.

Cluster volunteering

Recruit an entire group as the volunteer unit. The group might include an entire family, a club, or even a business. The group subdivides the work, lessening the time burden on any single member. Start this process by recruiting one member of the group who will persuade the others to become involved, making the volunteer job their project.

Both of these approaches are substantiated by data from the J.C. Penny survey of volunteer involvement. In that study, 71% of non-volunteers said they would be attracted by a volunteer opportunity in which they could work with friends or peers, and 55% said they would be interested in an opportunity to do volunteer work with their families. By giving them these opportunities, you are essentially creating 'two-fers', positions in which the volunteer can simultaneously do good and spend time with others.

Your search for volunteer groups may lead you into some strange places. Consider, for example, Lifers Group, Inc, a volunteer club that operates out of East Jersey State Prison. The convicts have established a group that helps local organisations raise money and other resources. High school students in Philadelphia have formed a group to provide volunteer computer assistance to local organisations and other students; they call the programme 'Dial-a-Nerd.'

Management of these 'volunteer clusters' will depend upon your

---

A demonstration project on family volunteering conducted by VOLUNTEER: The National Centre suggested the following characteristics for design of successful family volunteer jobs:

◆ The time commitment is flexible, often beginning with one-shot or short-term jobs that have the potential to grow into continuing activities.

◆ The jobs have understandable goals and logical, specific activities to be undertaken.

◆ The jobs provide something relevant for every member of the family.

◆ The jobs take advantage of the unique nature of family relationships.

◆ The jobs provide an opportunity to work with other volunteers, particularly other families.

utilising an existing natural leader of the group as your key supervisory mechanism. The group must enforce its own rules, and will resist too much direct outside intervention. Make sure that you have worked out a way of relating to the group leader, and use them to train and direct the group.

Groups may often rotate leadership, as does 'doing something', a volunteer group for young professionals in Washington, DC: *'Volunteers are encouraged to take the lead on a project that interests them and to coordinate the activities of the project. By rotating responsibilities, the group avoids letting one volunteer take on too much, and acts as a safeguard against burnout.'*

Ease them in

One of the reasons for saying 'No' to a high-time or high-involvement position is that the volunteer is afraid. This fear might be based on a feeling that the volunteer won't like the job enough to devote the time and energy to it, that it isn't worth the investment which it requires on the part of the volunteer. It might equally be based on a fear that the volunteer won't be able to do the job well enough, and a reluctance to let the organisation down.

Both of these difficulties can be dealt with by introducing the volunteer to the position gradually rather than expecting them to buy the whole package at once. Here are some ways to let the volunteer become accustomed to the more difficult position:

Test driving

Offer the potential volunteer a 30 day trial period. Tell them to try the job and see if they like it enough to keep it. This approach both allows the volunteer to see if they like the job and the organisation to see if they like the volunteer.

Schedule a review meeting when the volunteer starts the position and stress that the volunteer is under no obligation to continue the job after the test period — a 'no fault' divorce clause. While you will lose some volunteers, you will gain quite a few who have had the opportunity to examine the job without pressure, learned that they liked the work, and decided that investing their time and energy was worth it.

The test drive system works quite well because most of us are accustomed to dealing with it in other parts of our lives. Would you, for example, buy a car without taking it for a drive? Would you buy a new and unfamiliar product that didn't have a money back guarantee?

The implicit promise to the volunteer is *'Try it, you'll like it!'* And the reassurance is that the volunteer can honourably back away if they don't feel as though they really do like the job. At that point, however, the resourceful volunteer coordinator will try to negotiate with them about another job with the organisation...a smart move in this case, since anyone can persuade someone to volunteer *once*, the skill is to find them a job they will stick with and enjoy.

Apprenticeships

Apprenticeships work by making the volunteer an aide to the person who is currently holding the job. The volunteer then operates as an assistant at the direction of the volunteer who is presently responsible for performing that position.

Apprenticeships work exceptionally well for leadership jobs or jobs with large amounts of responsibility which people are reluctant to take because they don't feel totally comfortable about being able to do the work well. Examples of good positions for considering apprenticeships are chairs of committees or special events, or technical jobs which require decision-making experience which the volunteer does not currently possess.

During the apprenticeship they can learn to do the work until they are comfortable with their ability to handle it well. At the end of the apprenticeship they can be 'recognised' by a promotion to being in charge, a position which they will now think they have earned and for which they will now think they are prepared.

A variation on apprenticeship is the 'mentor' or 'buddy' system. In these cases, the assisting senior volunteer does not directly supervise the new volunteer but serves to provide advice as requested or needed, and often will operate as a coach to the newcomer.

Propinquity

This method works through obtaining a volunteer for a difficult position by first recruiting them for something else instead. This might sound a bit strange if you don't understand the propinquity principle.

'Propinquity' is the process of becoming accustomed to and favourably disposed toward those things or people which you are around and used to, somewhat to the effect 'familiarity breeds affection.'

Things, or people, or jobs which seemed too large or too difficult or too frightening because they were new or strange may no longer seem quite so daunting after you've been around them for a while.

In propinquity recruitment, you attempt to recruit a person for an alternate position which is near or connected to the position for which you eventually want them to serve.

For example, if your organisation was having trouble recruiting counsellors for one-to-one work with emotionally disturbed children, you might recruit someone to assist in collecting data from the volunteers currently doing that job. Data collection is a small and simple job that is easily done, but while doing it the volunteer is exposed to the more difficult job and can learn to understand it and how valuable it is. Through the process of propinquity, data collection volunteers are more likely to become attached to the counselling job with which they are in contact. When then asked to consider becoming counsellors they are more likely not to be as afraid of the position, thinking *'If those guys can do it, so can I.'*

One way to view recruitment by propinquity is that you are simply creating a new population of 'concentric circle' volunteers who will become interested in the job. Another way is to view it as the 'bait and switch' approach to the problem. By any way that you view it, it works: people are much less reluctant to take jobs that they understand and are accustomed to. In recruitment by propinquity, the job ends up speaking for itself.

IDENTIFYING POTENTIAL RECRUITMENT APPEALS

All of the above methods for volunteer recruitment require that the recruiter develop a message that explains what the organisation is offering to the volunteer, and which will tap some motivational impulse of that volunteer. The possible range of volunteer motivations is very broad, encompassing practically every psychological attribute. This tends to lead organisations to develop very broad motivational appeals, believing that someone amongst all those potential volunteers will respond to them. It is important, however, to realise that what is needed in the development of the recruitment appeal is a slightly narrower approach, motivating potential volunteers not just to decide, in general, to volunteer, but to volunteer with this particular organisation, doing this particular job.

To create a more defined appeal, the organisation should develop answers to four key questions which can be communicated to the potential volunteer:

- **Why should this job be done at all?**
  What is the need in the community for this work? What problems will arise if this volunteer job is not done?

- **What will the benefit be to the community or to the clientele if the job is done?**
  What will the work accomplish? What changes will it make in people's lives?

- **What are some possible fears or objections concerning this job which must be overcome?**
  The type of clients? The subject area? The skills needed to do the work? Geography?

- **What will be the personal benefit to the volunteer in doing the job?**
  Skills? Experience? Flexible work schedules? New friends?

The appeal can then focus on communicating to the potential volunteer why the organisation and its work are important, and why the potential volunteer should contribute to the accomplishment of that work. Different aspects of this message may be stressed more than others, or may be communicated differently in different recruitment drives. An appeal to young people, for example, might stress job experience possibilities, while an appeal to previous clients of the organisation may talk about the effects of the problem and the ability to help others obtain the relief that they themselves have experienced.

Creating an effective message is much more difficult than it seems, particularly when this is being done by paid employees. Quite often their own extensive knowledge of the organisation and its work interferes with writing an effective appeal; in a sense they are too familiar with the subject to remember that others lack that basic knowledge. They will often forget to include the most basic of facts - numbers of persons in the community who face the problem; harmful effects of the condition - because they 'assume' that others in the community are as familiar with the situation as they are. Their own intimate relationship with the situation makes them think that others are equally aware. This means that field-testing of recruitment appeals is quite important, to make sure that the general population receives the appropriate information in a way which they can both understand and relate to. (*See over the page suggestions on your recruitment message*).

STARTING A RECRUITMENT CAMPAIGN

As this chapter indicates, there are a lot of possible ways to engage in recruitment. The smart volunteer manager will pick and choose methods depending on the desired results:

♦ **A warm body campaign** is good for when you need a large amount of volunteers for an event, or when you are just beginning a programme and need to attract community attention.

♦ **A targeted recruitment campaign** is good for finding individuals with specific talents or interests.

♦ **A concentric circle campaign** is good for maintaining a steady flow of replacement volunteers.

Each type of campaign can successfully recruit volunteers; the trick is to select the campaign that will obtain the right types of volunteers with the least amount of effort.

Each campaign, however, is dependent upon identifying possible motivational appeals that individuals might have and connecting these motivations to some volunteer opportunity that your organisation has to offer.

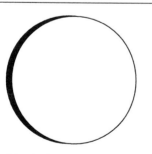

This circle represents the motivational needs of individuals that might be tapped in recruitment campaigns.

SUGGESTIONS FOR PUTTING AN EFFECTIVE MESSAGE INTO WRITING:

1 The opening of the message is interesting enough to entice the potential volunteer to continue reading or listening.

2 The body of the message is appealing enough to interest the potential volunteer in considering the volunteer opportunity or, at least, in contacting the organisation to get more information. Boring messages are only likely to appeal to boring people.

3 The body of the message presents information in an order that psychologically matches how people will think about the offer:

◆ **Need:** *Is there a problem?*

◆ **Solution:** *Can this job help solve it?*

◆ **Fears/Questions:** *Will I be capable of helping with it?*

◆ **Benefits:** *What's in it for me?*

◆ **Contact Point:** *How do I get involved?*

As a general rule, spend more space on need than on logistics. People will first decide whether you're worth volunteering for and then decide whether they can fit you into their schedule. The need you stress may be yours, your clientele's, or a perceived need/benefit for the volunteer.

4 The message is easily understood. The message is intelligible and avoids jargon, unless it is included for a specific reason.

5 The message has been tested for ease of comprehension by someone other than the author of the Message. Remember: *What can be misunderstood, will be.*

6 The message gives a complete picture: problem, type of work, requirements, time-frame, person to talk with. The message doesn't make the potential volunteer have to do any extra work in order to understand what is going on.

7 The contact information for the message gives the name of a person, preferably including their first name, not just the name of the organisation. Volunteering is a personal decision and people like to talk with other people about it.

Topics covered include:

◆ **Purposes of interviewing**

◆ **Organising the interview - interviewer & location**

◆ **Preparation for the interview**

◆ **The effective interview**

◆ **Matching the volunteers to jobs**

Effective volunteer interviewing and screening is essential to good practice in volunteer management but is often neglected. This chapter covers specific techniques as well as policies relevant to screening and interviewing volunteers.

One of the most neglected areas of volunteer management training has been that of effective interviewing of volunteers. This is unfortunate, since good interviewing skills are essential to performing that most crucial of all volunteer management tasks – matching a potential volunteer with a task and a working environment that they will enjoy.

Even more unfortunate is the fact that much of the management training which does exist on interviewing deals with employment interviewing, which is actually a totally inappropriate approach for volunteer interviewing. The main difference is quite easily stated: volunteer interviewing consists of evaluating a person for a job, not for the job. Effective volunteer interviewing does not so much consist of examining an applicant's suitability for one job as it does evaluating the ability and desire of that applicant to fit productively in some position within the organisation. Employment interviewing focuses on the question, *'Who can do this job?'*, while volunteer interviewing should focus on the more creative question, *'Who will want to do this job?'* Ivan Scheier called this 'the people approach' over twenty years ago, and that phrase still exemplifies the proper attitude to the process.

PURPOSES OF VOLUNTEER SCREENING

Among other things this difference in approach means that a volunteer interview has to accomplish more than the usual job interview. There are two basic purposes:

◆ Identify a 'fit'

This includes determining the interests and abilities of the potential volunteer, determining their suitability for particular jobs, and assessing their 'rightness' for the organisation, its style of operation, and its mission. 'Fit' is the interpersonal matching of the needs and interests of the volunteer with the needs and interests of the organisation. An examination of proper fit would include determining these items regarding the volunteer:

1 To what extent does the volunteer have both an interest in a particular job and the necessary qualifications to perform that job?

2 To what extent does the volunteer have other interests and abilities that might be used to create a different job for them?

3 To what extent does the volunteer have a 'rightness' for working well in a particular job environment.

In many cases, 'rightness,' which involves the likelihood that the volunteer will fit comfortably into the organisation, working environment, will be the key predictive factor for success. Rightness could involve questions of style (relaxed, frenetic), personality (neat, messy; introverted, extroverted), behaviour (smoking, non-smoking), political philosophy (traditionalist, radical), or other items which would affect how the volunteer will get along, both with the organisation in general and with that particular staff group to whom they might be assigned. Very often these interpersonal relationship factors become more important than factors of technical qualification, which can be learned if the volunteer is willing to stay with the organisation. Quite simply, a volunteer who is happy in his or her working environment will make the job happen; one who is unhappy will not try to do so.

◆ Recruit

This includes answering any questions or concerns that the potential volunteer may have and persuading the volunteer of his or her ability to make a contribution to the organisation and its clientele, or that s/he will derive personal satisfaction from helping. It is a quite mistaken belief that the person who shows up for an interview has already decided to volunteer with the organisation.

During the process of the interview, it is crucial to remember that the volunteer has not yet been recruited. At this stage they have only been 'attracted' to the organisation. One purpose of the screening interview is to give the volunteer the time to make a more deliberate examination of what the organisation has to offer and to have a chance to 'sell' the organisation and its work to the volunteer. Equal time has to be given to focusing on 'why' a particular job is important and interesting, as well as to whether the volunteer would be right for that job. Never assume that just because a volunteer has come to the interview, that they are already a part of the organisation. If the screening interview is your first contact with the volunteer, then it is important that the volunteer feels welcomed and wanted during the interview process, and does not feel as though they have already been caught by an uncaring bureaucracy which is only interested in determining which Square Hole the volunteer should fill.

A number of abilities are desirable in a volunteer interviewer:

◆ Broad knowledge of the organisation and its programmes

◆ Personal knowledge of staff and their quirks

◆ Ability to relate to all types of people

◆ Ability to talk easily with strangers

◆ Ability to listen attentively both to what is said and is not said

◆ Ability to ask follow-up questions

◆ Ability to follow the agenda of the interview without appearing to dominate

◆ Knowledge of non-directive interview techniques

◆ Ability to recruit and motivate while interviewing

◆ Commitment to the organisation and its programmes

◆ Ability to empathise with other people

◆ Ability to say 'no'

PICKING AN INTERVIEWER

Since the time available for assessing potential candidates for volunteer positions is relatively short, it is important to have a person conducting the interviews who is capable of making a satisfactory judgment.

Volunteers often make better interviewers than paid staff. This is true for two reasons. First, they tend not to be 'burned out' in interviewing because they may be involved in a lesser number. Conducting interviews is a draining process, and one which can easily become overwhelming. The common response in this situation is to stop listening after a while. Second, volunteers tend to be better able to build a rapport with potential volunteers, because, after all, they have something important in common – each thought the organisation was worth donating their time to.

THE INTERVIEWING SITE

Since a volunteer interview requires a greater exploration of personal characteristics, site selection can be critical. Three factors are important:

◆ Accessibility

◆ A friendly atmosphere

◆ Privacy

The site for conducting the interview will vary, but it is important during the interview that the volunteer feels a sense of privacy and comfort. Do not conduct the interview in a public place or in a shared office, since this will deter many volunteers from offering complete information about their backgrounds and their interests. None of us likes being eavesdropped on while discussing our personal lives.

Organise your own schedule so that you will not be interrupted during the interview, either by phone calls or by other staff. Besides disrupting the flow of the interview, interruptions give the impression to the volunteer that they are of a much lesser importance than your other work.

Remember the old adage: *'You never get a second chance to make a first impression'*. What the potential volunteer sees and feels during the interview may shape their eventual attitude toward the organisation.

PRE-INTERVIEW PREPARATION

The following items should be prepared and ready before the interview:

◆ A list of possible volunteer jobs, with descriptions of work and qualifications required .

◆ A list of questions to be asked in relation to each job.

◆ A application form completed by the volunteer with background information about them and their interest in you.

◆ A set of open-ended questions to explore the motivations of the volunteer.

◆ Information and materials on the organisation and its work programmes.

OPENING THE INTERVIEW

The beginning of the interview should focus on:

◆ Making the applicant feel welcome. Express appreciation for them coming to meet you.

◆ Building rapport. Explain what you would like to accomplish and how they fit into the process. Let them know that their decision about whether volunteering with you would be suitable is the aim of the discussion. Let them feel 'in charge.'

◆ Giving them background information about the organisation and its work. Ask them what questions they have about the organisation and its purpose and programmes.

The key to beginning a successful interview is to start building rapport with the potential volunteer. It is crucial that the interview process belongs as much to the volunteer as it does to the organisation. If there is a time limit for the interview, make sure that you have allocated sufficient time for the volunteer to express concerns and ask questions. The interview should be a mutual, not unilateral, information exchange process. It is a negotiation, not an interrogation. Make sure that you explain to the volunteer at the beginning of the interview that they should feel free to ask questions and express any concerns at any point during the discussion.

CONDUCTING THE INTERVIEW

The major portion of the interview should be devoted to the following:

♦ Exploration of the applicant's interests, abilities, and personal situation. Determine why the applicant is considering volunteering and what types of work environment they prefer.

♦ Discussion of various job possibilities. Explain the purpose and work situation of the different volunteer job opportunities available and let the applicant consider them. Use this as an opportunity to let the applicant discuss how they would approach various jobs, which will tell you more about their attitudes, their intentions and their level of interest.

♦ Discuss your requirements: time commitments, training requirements, paperwork, confidentiality rules, etc. Let the volunteer know what will be expected of them.

♦ Remember that you are still 'recruiting' the volunteer at this stage, so do not forget to explain why each job is important to the interests of the organisation and the clientele.

♦ Look for personality indicators that will help you match this person to a situation where they will be happy. This can include items such as whether they smoke, desire for individual or group work, and other preferences.

One of the important skills to possess during the interview is the ability to detect an unexpected talent in the volunteer and to begin to construct a possible volunteer role for them on the spot. This requires a good understanding of the organisation and its work. If you make use of volunteers to conduct interviews (where they may be very effective is in building a rapport and seeing things from the viewpoint of the potential volunteer) make sure they have a good background about the organisation and how its work is organised.

Here are some examples of questions which can be used during the interview:

◆ 'What can I tell you about our organisation?'

◆ 'What attracted you to our organisation? Is there any aspect of our work that most motivates you to seek to volunteer here?'

◆ 'What would you like to get out of volunteering here? What will make you feel like your volunteering has been successful?'

◆ 'What have you enjoyed most or least about your previous volunteer work? About your paid employment?'

◆ 'Describe your ideal supervisor. How do you prefer that supervisor to relate to you?'

◆ 'Would you rather work on your own, with a group, or with a partner? Why?'

◆ 'What skills do you think you have to contribute?'

◆ 'How would you spend the day if you could go anywhere and do anything?'

◆ 'Are there any types of clients that you would most prefer to work with? Or that you would not feel comfortable working with?

◆ 'What do you think is the most important thing we should be doing to help our clients and to fulfil our mission in the community?'

◆ 'How do you think you would go about this volunteer assignment? Where would you start and what do you think are the most important considerations?'

◆ 'Give me an example.'

◆ 'Why do you think that was the case?'

While it is important to evaluate different elements for different volunteer jobs, here are some general areas to watch for while interviewing:

- Ease in answering questions about personal qualifications and background
- Ability to communicate well
- Level of enthusiasm and commitment
- General attitudes and emotional reactions
- Types of questions asked about the organisation and the position on offer
- Other interests of hobbies
- Flexibility
- Maturity and stability
- Preference for a group or individual setting for volunteer work
- Level of self-confidence
- Any sense of a hidden agenda
- Time pattern of previous work and volunteer experience
- Reasons for coming to the interview
- Preferences in type of work

CLOSING THE INTERVIEW

The interview should be concluded by:

- Making an offer of a possible position to the volunteer, or politely explaining that you have no suitable openings for them at this time.

- Explaining what will happen next: making background or reference checks, arranging a second interview with staff, scheduling a training or induction session, etc. Explain the process, the timeframe, and what is expected of the volunteer at each stage.

- Explaining the next steps in the process: what will happen, and by when.

- Getting the permission of the volunteer to conduct any reference or background checks.

OTHER INTERVIEW CONSIDERATIONS

Face-to-face or over the telephone?

Some programmes are simply not in a position to conduct interviews in person. This is not a common situation but it obviously makes the recruitment process less personal and inhibits both the ability of the organisation to evaluate the volunteer and the volunteer to assess the organisation. Generally speaking, it is highly desirable to conduct face-to-face interviews for job situations which have the following attributes:

◆ The job requires a longer time commitment and thus a higher motivational level on the part of the volunteer.

◆ The job entails greater responsibility or requires a capacity or skill above the ordinary.

◆ The job possesses high sensitivity because of the nature of the work or the relationship with clients.

If you are unable to conduct a personal interview for a job which involves any one of these characteristics, it is highly desirable to schedule a 30-day review with the volunteer to see how they are performing and how they are feeling.

Reference checks

It may also be important to conduct a check of a potential volunteer's credentials. This is particularly important in cases where the volunteer position requires licensing or certification or where it involves working with a clientele with diminished capacities. If you are going to check an applicants references, it is important to notify them and obtain their permission. One way

OVERALL INTERVIEW SUGGESTIONS

◆ Make sure your interview time is not interrupted. This will make it much easier for the interviewer and the candidate to be comfortable.

◆ Be an active listener. You need to understand the candidate and that requires paying very close attention both to what they are saying and what they are not saying during the interview.

◆ Answer any questions about the organisation and its work openly and honestly. This will both demonstrate your sincerity and your intelligence. You can't hide things from people who will start working with the organisation and will therefore find out eventually anyway.

◆ Don't promise anything if you are not sure of being able to make a placement. Never promise anything that you can't deliver to the volunteer.

◆ Describe the volunteer position honestly. Do not hide undesirable aspects of the job in the hope that the volunteer won't mind discovering them after they've signed on.

◆ Evaluate people on an individual basis. Don't assume they're like anyone else that you've ever met.

to do so is by having them sign a permission document such as the following:

SAMPLE PERMISSION DOCUMENT TO BE SIGNED BY VOLUNTEER:

I hereby allow [name of organisation] to perform a check of my background, including

◆ Police record

◆ Driving record

◆ Past employment/volunteer history

◆ Financial history

◆ Educational/professional status

◆ Personal references

◆ Physician or therapist

◆ And other persons or sources as appropriate for the volunteer jobs in which I have expressed an interest.

I understand that I do not have to agree to this background check, but that refusal to do so may exclude me from consideration for some types of volunteer work.

I understand that information collected during this background check will be limited to that appropriate to determining my suitability for particular types of volunteer work and that all such information collected during the check will be kept confidential.

I hereby also extend my permission to those individuals or organisations contacted for the purpose of this background check to give their full and honest evaluation of my suitability of the described volunteer work and such other information as they deem appropriate.

Note that not all types of references would need to be checked for each volunteer. What needs to be checked relates to a particular volunteer position.

Involving staff in volunteer interviewing

It is crucial that the staff who have responsibility for overseeing the job which the volunteer will be performing have some involvement in the interviewing process. That involvement might take several forms:

◆ *Assisting in writing questions and scenarios for use during the interview.*

This is a vital function where staff are more familiar with the demands and requirements of a particular job than the volunteer coordinator.

◆ *Participating in the actual interview.*

While this is possible, it is not normally recommended. The difficulty this creates is that it limits the ability of the volunteer interviewer to negotiate with the potential volunteer about more than one job. Instead, we recommend that staff be involved in direct interviewing through conducting a second interview with potential volunteers, after preliminary ideas regarding placement have been made.

CONTRACTING

You may wish to consider initiating a process of entering into a contract with volunteers once the interviewing and matching process has been satisfactorily concluded. Contracting does not actually involve a formal legal document, as much as it does the signing by both the organisation and the volunteer of a listing of the mutual commitments and intentions they are entering into. The agreement might specify the work which the volunteer is agreeing to perform, the timeframe, and the benefits and support which the organisation agrees to provide the volunteer.

The purpose of the contract is to emphasise the seriousness of both the organisation and the volunteer in entering into a relationship, and is not intended to convey a sense of 'legal' responsibility. Contracts work particularly well with young volunteers.

MATCHING VOLUNTEERS TO POSITIONS

Determining the correct job for a volunteer involves questions of both qualifications and temperament. The volunteer must certainly be capable of doing or learning to do the job for which they are selected. But it is equally important that the volunteer 'fits' into the work situation. This means that the volunteer must be satisfied with the job being offered, and views the job as providing desirable and fulfilling work. It means that the work setting (including the hours and location of the job) must also be acceptable to the volunteer. And finally it means that the staff or other volunteers with whom the volunteer will be working must also be suitable. This last factor may ultimately be decided by some relatively 'personal' factors, such as compatibility or personality type, style of work, or even whether one person

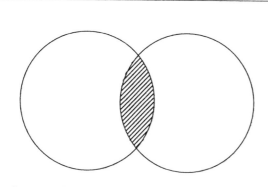

These circles represent the interests of the organisation and of the volunteer. The volunteer interview is designed to identify that area of overlap in which a volunteer job can be designed that satisfies both parties.

smokes and the other doesn't. The purpose of this matching operation is to identify areas of common interest and common satisfaction, as well as potential areas of friction or difficulty.

Since it is difficult to make totally accurate decisions in a 30-minute interview, it is desirable to offer all 'assignments' on a trial-period basis. Let the volunteer know that the first thirty days of work will be done as a probationary period for both the volunteer and the organisation. At the end of the thirty days, a second 'interview' will be conducted in which both parties will re-evaluate the assignment. During this subsequent interview either party may request a change of assignment, based upon their additional knowledge of the situation.

This initial testing period will both make it easier to encourage volunteers to try out jobs about which they are uncertain. It will also be more likely that any problems of mis-matching will be identified early and corrected quickly.

CHAPTER SIX

ORIENTATION & TRAINING

Topics covered include:

◆ **Orienting the volunteers when they first arrive.**

◆ **Providing the training they will need in information, skills, and approaches to the work.**

◆ **Encouraging and facilitating volunteer learning on the job.**

◆ **Providing future training opportunities as a volunteer benefit.**

Your volunteers are a valuable resource. The value of their time is a significant benefit to the organisation. Their contribution helps the organisation achieve its goals. This chapter is all about investing in your volunteers to improve their performance and enhance the contribution they make.

Every volunteer needs some level of induction for their work with the organisation. This preparation falls into two parts:

◆ **Orientation,** the process of preparing the volunteer for a clear relationship with the organisation (also known as induction).

◆ **Training,** the process of preparing the volunteer to perform work for the organisation.

Every volunteer should know they will be required to attend an orientation and/or training session. Orientation may be distinguished from training in that it is usually more general in nature, providing information every volunteer should know. Training is designed to equip volunteers with skills and knowledge required by their specific positions.

ORIENTATION

Even if volunteers come to the job with all the skills necessary to do the job, they will need some orientation to the organisation. Orientation is the process of making volunteers feel comfortable with and understand the workings of the organisation. It is designed to provide them with background and practical knowledge of the organisation and to let them understand how they can contribute to the purpose of the organisation. If the volunteer better understands the organisation's systems, operations, and procedures, s/he will be able to contribute more productively.

There are three different subject areas which should be covered during the orientation process:

❶ **The cause.**

❷ **The systems for volunteer management.**

❸ **The social environment for the volunteer.**

Cause orientation

This area involves introducing the volunteer to the purpose of the organisation. It should cover:

◆ A description of the problem or cause

◆ A description of the client group

◆ A description of the mission and values of the organisation

◆ A description of the history of the organisation

◆ A description of the programmes and service of the organisation

◆ A description of other groups working in the same field, and their distinguishing characteristics from this organisation

◆ A description of future plans of the organisation

The presentation of these items should be a discussion rather than a dry description. The intention of this portion of the orientation is to allow the volunteer to begin to learn and join the basic values of the organisation. Part of this will involve possible debate over the philosophy and approach the organisation is taking to solve its identified community need; part may involve learning the myths and legends of the organisation through hearing stories about early leaders.

The goal of this discussion is to allow the volunteer to make an intellectual and emotional commitment to the basic purpose of the organisation, to make a conscious decision that they believe in and are willing to work toward achieving the mission of the organisation. This portion of the orientation is intended to allow the volunteer to 'join the cause.'

System orientation

This portion of the orientation involves introducing the volunteer to the system of volunteer management with the organisation. It would include presentation and discussion of:

◆ The structure and programmes of the organisation, with illustrations of what volunteers contribute to those programmes.

◆ The system of volunteer involvement within the organisation: policies and procedures.

◆ An introduction to facilities and equipment.

◆ A description of volunteer requirements and benefits.

◆ An introduction to recordkeeping requirements.

◆ A description of the timing of the organisation's activities and key events.

The simplest way to develop the agenda for this portion of the orientation session is to ask yourself *'What would I like to know about this place in order to better understand how it works?'* Remember that friends will ask the volunteers about their volunteer work and about the organisation. A volunteer who fully understands the organisation can well serve as an effective communicator with the public about the worth of the organisation, while a confused volunteer can present quite the opposite picture.

The purpose of this portion of the orientation session is to provide an organisational context for the volunteer and make them understand how they fit into the processes of the organisation. This material is often presented in a factual way, with charts and descriptive handouts, followed by a question and answer period to clarify issues. It can be made more lively by having different representatives, both paid and volunteer, describe varying aspects of the work of the organisation. The goal of this part of the orientation session is to allow the volunteer to see how they will fit into helping address the need; it identifies the role they will be playing in the work of the organisation, the basic requirements of that role, and how that role links to other areas of the organisation.

Social orientation

This portion of the orientation introduces the volunteer to the social community which they are being asked to join and begins to forge the personal bonds that will sustain volunteer involvement.

Included in this introduction are:

◆ An introduction to the leadership of the organisation (you must decide who could best present or lead part of the discussion on the mission of the organisation).

◆ A 'welcoming' by staff and current volunteers (through their participation in presenting subject areas or even as a purely social occasion).

◆ A description of the culture and etiquette of the organisation (matters such as dress, customs, etc.)

This part of the orientation session can proceed in a variety of ways. It might be interspersed throughout the other stages of orientation, with official greeting, welcoming, and presentation serving to initiate personal contacts. It might begin right after formal acceptance of a volunteer, with the assignment of a personal mentor or companion who contacts the volunteers, meets with them informally to welcome them to the organisation and introduce them to its processes, and then supports them during their early involvement. It might consist of introducing the volunteer to their future supervisor and arranging for a discussion about how they will be working together. It might consist of a welcoming party for a new volunteer hosted by staff and current volunteers.

The purpose of this part of the orientation is to show the volunteer who they will be working with, and welcoming them into the social context of the organisation. The goal is to show the volunteer that they are a welcome addition to the 'team.'

These aspects of orientation are designed to answer three basic questions for the new volunteer:

◆ **Cause Orientation:**
Why should I be working here?

◆ **System Orientation:**
How will I be working here?

◆ **Social Orientation:**
How do I fit in with everyone else?

The importance of orientation

These three questions *(left)* are crucial if the volunteer is to feel comfortable. A volunteer who does not 'feel' right about these three aspects of volunteering will cease to feel a part of the organisation. Much of the early retention loss in some volunteer programmes is due to the absence of a good orientation. Orientation should 'seal the deal' between the organisation and the volunteer, clearly establishing the intellectual, practical, and emotional bonds between the two.

Some organisations avoid giving time to orientation because of difficulty in getting volunteers to attend. This problem can be addressed. It might require altering the scheduling of orientations, placing them on weekends or during the evening. It might involve altering the format of orientations, doing them one-on-one, in small groups, or in several shorter sessions. It might require making attendance mandatory, even if that means losing some potential volunteers. Make whatever adjustments are necessary, and ensure that all new volunteers receive a proper orientation.

Perhaps the best way of understanding the importance of orientation is simply to consider its basic definition. 'Orientation' is the process of learning one's direction and bearings in the world; a person without orientation is, to put it simply, 'lost.'

TRAINING

Training is the process of providing volunteers with the ability to perform specific types of work.

Design of training

Determining what training a volunteer may need requires answers to three questions:

♦ What *information* do they need to successfully perform the work?

♦ What *skills* do they need to successfully perform the work?

♦ What *attitudes* or *approaches* do they need to successfully perform the work?

Training to provide this information, develop these skills and engender these attitudes can be provided in three formats: formal training sessions, coaching sessions, and counselling.

Formal training

Formal training will prepare volunteers for specific jobs. Sometimes this training can be quite lengthy, particularly when volunteers are recruited who lack the specific job skills required by the position. Crisis Lines, for example, provide many hours of training in how to deal with callers. These hours may be spread over a couple of weeks. One programme for counselling delinquent children requires one evening per week of training for a year before the volunteers begin work with clients. Volunteer firefighters in the US typically attend training once a week to polish up and expand their skills for as long as they are with the fire department.

Training can be presented through lectures, readings, discussions, field trips, videos, panel discussions, demonstrations, role-play, case studies, simulations, and more. Trainers commonly employ a variety of techniques so as to retain the attention of the audience.

There are two primary content areas to cover in volunteer training, regardless of the job for which the training is being provided. The first area is a *description of the functions of the volunteer job* to communicate to the volunteer:

❶ *This is what you should do and accomplish in your job*

❷ *This is what you should not do*

❸ *This is what you should do in the following situations*

A volunteer who is recruited to drive elderly clients to medical appointments might be trained as follows:

❶ **Do:**
be on time or notify the programme coordinator at least three hours in advance if you are going to be late; help patients in and out of the car; be familiar with the city; have a roadworthy and insured vehicle; use the recommended method of assisting patients from a wheelchair into the vehicle; follow the correct steps in folding and storing a wheelchair.

❷ **Don't:**
volunteer to assist clients with in-home chores; offer to take clients to other appointments on an unscheduled basis; take clients shopping; tell clients about the medical conditions of others; offer medical advice.

❸ **If:**
if there is a medical problem en route, go immediately to the nearest emergency room, the locations of which are marked on your map; if the client asks for your opinion of his or her doctor, tell the client you aren't qualified to make such a judgment.

The content of the training provides the volunteer with the collected experience (both positive and negative) that previous volunteers have acquired. The content should be developed with the assistance of staff and volunteers who are familiar with the work, and the session might be delivered by these same staff or volunteers.

The second area might be termed a description of roles and responsibilities. It would include training which communicates to the volunteer the web of relationships in which they will be working:

❶ *This is with whom you will be working and this is your role in the task.*

❷ *This is their role and how it fits into the task.*

For example, this could include telling volunteers who their supervisor will be and any other staff or volunteers who will be assigned to work in concert with them. For example, a volunteer working with others to serve a particular client should be introduced to those volunteers and learn what each is providing to that client and how their efforts dovetail.

Coaching

Coaching is a process of teaching or upgrading skills. It can be used in formal training sessions or in on-the-job training. It will most often be provided by the supervisor of the volunteer or a more experienced co-worker. Effective coaching follows a three-step process:

❶ A demonstration of the skill to be learned or improved

❷ Observation of the volunteer trying out the skill

❸ Feedback and analysis

The skill can be demonstrated by anyone expert in that area. Either the person demonstrating the skill or the coach (supervisor, trainer, or volunteer programme manager) should explain why the expert is doing it. The point of the demonstration is not just to allow the volunteer to see what is being done but to understand it.

To take an extremely simple example, if you were to demonstrate to a volunteer how to answer the organisation telephone, you might have the volunteer watch you answer the phone a few times. Then you might observe the volunteer answering the phone. Third, you might have the volunteer answer the phone without being observed. After each stage you would discuss the experience with the intention that the volunteer learns from it.

The EIAG process

To increase your chances of the volunteer learning, these discussions can follow a learning model called EIAG. Although this doesn't spell anything, the four letters are the initial letters in the four major steps people go through to learn things. If you keep these steps in mind as you coach volunteers, you can make sure they get the most from the learning process.

THE EIAG PROCESS

❶ **E** - Experience

❷ **I** - Identify

❸ **A** - Analyse

❹ **G** - Generalise

Experience

The 'E' stands for *experience*. People learn from experiences, be they training exercises or real world events. But not always. Sometimes people have the same experience over and over again and never learn anything from it. If a person is to learn from an experience, their minds go through three additional steps.

Identify

The 'I' is for *identify*. If a person is to learn from an experience, they have to be able to describe it. In the simple example of learning to answer the phone above, some questions you might ask at the various steps to get someone to describe the experience are:

◆ *What did I do?*

◆ *What did you do?*

◆ *How did the other person react?*

◆ *How have things been going for you?*

◆ *What has been happening?*

Analyse

The third step in learning from experience is to *analyse* it. You want to get the volunteer to explore the factors in the situation that produced the experience. To continue with the example, some questions you might ask are:

◆ *Why did I begin by saying 'Good morning?'*

◆ *What advantages are there to giving your name?*

◆ *Why did the caller get so upset with you?*

◆ *Why have things been going so well?*

Generalise

The 'G' stands for *generalise*. If a person is to learn anything useful from an experience, s/he must be able to come up with some general rule or principle that applies beyond the specific situation to other, similar situations. Again, an effective coach relies on questions in this step. Some examples are:

◆ *What will you do when you encounter a situation like this?*

◆ *What would you do differently if you had to do it over again?*

◆ *What would you advise someone else who is about to do this?*

◆ *What will you do to make sure things continue going so well?*

As you begin to use the EIAG model, *(an example of which can be seen overleaf)* it is important that the sequence of questions you use be natural. Sometimes you may have a tendency to get locked into our prepared sequence of questions while a volunteer's response might naturally bring up other questions. If you have prepared a series of identification questions, don't ask them all in a row if you get an unexpected response on the first one. It might be better to go on and analyse that response than to proceed with your other questions.

The EIAG coaching model is effective because it is a natural one. It merely makes conscious the subconscious method you employ all the time. When you employ it, you are merely making sure that your volunteers complete all the steps in the learning process instead of leaving it to chance that they will do it on their own.

It also enables you to spot erroneous conclusions volunteers might reach from their limited experience. Look at the example overleaf: if Michael, for example, generalises that *'Johnny is simply incapable of learning anything,'* you might respond by getting him to analyse that statement: *'Why do you say that?'* You might give him sympathy for the difficulty of the task and encouragement to try harder. But above all you need to bring him to a different generalisation based on the facts, asking questions such as:

◆ *Is there anything else in the situation that might have caused that problem?*

◆ *What does seem to get Johnny's attention?*

◆ *Can you think of any way to use that in the lesson?*

◆ *What will you try tomorrow?*

AN EXAMPLE OF EIAG
• EXPERIENCE • IDENTIFITY • ANALYSE • GENERALISE •

Let's see how this might work in a more complex example. As stated previously, coaching is particularly important with a volunteer who is new to a skill or concept. Imagine, for example, that you are a teacher of handicapped children and that you have a volunteer named Michael. You want Michael to help a child named Johnny learn to put his coat on and take it off. Although Michael has some experience in working with handicapped children, he has never done anything like this before. So you start by having Michael watch you work with Johnny. Afterwards, you use the EIAG technique to discuss things with Michael. Some questions you might ask include:

◆ What did you see me do with Johnny? (*identifying*)

◆ What problems did I encounter? (*identifying*)

◆ Why do you think these occurred? (*analysing*)

◆ What do you think you could do to avoid such problems? (*generalising*)

◆ What techniques seemed to work well? (*identifying*)

◆ Why did these techniques work better than others I tried? (*analysing*)

◆ Based on what you saw, what are some things you will avoid and some things you will do when you work with Johnny? (*generalising*)

Once you are confident that Michael has a grasp of what to do, you watch him carefully while he attempts to conduct the lesson. During this time, if it seems like Michael is doing something that will upset or harm Johnny in any way, you would of course interrupt and suggest a different course of action. Or you might take over the lesson again yourself. In any case, after Michael's attempts, you would again ask questions to help him learn and grown from his experience:

◆ How would you describe what happened? (*identifying*)

◆ Why did you put your coat on? (*analysing*)

◆ What were the strengths of your approach? (*analysing*)

◆ Why did Johnny slap the applesauce out of your hand? (*analysing*)

◆ Based on this insight, what will you do differently next time? (*generalising*)

In the course of this, you may need to go back and demonstrate the skill again, with Michael watching. You would then go back to watching him. Eventually, when you are comfortable that Michael has mastered the skill, you would allow him to work without watching. Nonetheless, you would continue to check on his progress from time to time, using the EIAG questions to make sure he is continuing to grow in his abilities. The checking would include direct observation and reports from Michael. Eventually, you would be comfortable enough to rely simply on Michael's observations.

As with coaching, the principal tool the effective manager employs in counselling is the question. The supervisor can use questions to help the volunteer do these things:

Identify the problem

◆ *What is going wrong?*

◆ *What exactly is happening?*

Identify the cause of the problem

◆ *Why is the problem occurring?*

◆ *What is causing the problem?*

◆ *What factors in the situation are producing the problem?*

Identify alternatives

◆ *What are the alternatives you have in this situation?*

◆ *What else could you do?*

◆ *Have you considered this course of action? (making a suggestion)*

◆ *What would happen if you tried that?*

◆ *Then what would happen?*

Identify a better course of action

◆ *What are the strengths and weaknesses of each alternative?*

◆ *What can you do to solve the problem?*

◆ *Why do you think that might work?*

Learn from their experiences

◆ *What can you do differently in the future to avoid this problem?*

◆ *What would you do differently if you had it to do over again?*

Counselling

The goal of counselling is to assist the volunteer in solving a problem or improving behaviour by getting the volunteer to acknowledge a difficulty and take responsibility for the improvement. While coaching shows volunteers how they might improve in job skills, counselling helps volunteers discover how to improve their performance.

The counselling process

When a volunteer encounters a problem with the work or during training, s/he may feel that the volunteer aspect of his or her life is no longer under control. When people feel a lack of control of an area, they get frustrated and their self-esteem suffers, both of which can lead to volunteer turnover. The goal of the counselling process is to restore a feeling of control in the volunteer's life by helping him or her find a course of action that will solve the problem.

Providing counselling

It is fine to offer suggestions when counselling, offering additional information or suggestions for courses of action that the volunteer might not see. In doing so, however, you should not be telling the volunteer what to do. Your role, in counselling, is to empower them to come up with their own solutions. In doing this, you need to get them to own the ideas that originate from you by having them analyse them. The conversation might go something like this:

◆ *'Have you considered this course of action?'*
'Oh, so that's what you want me to do?'

◆ *'Not necessarily. Have you considered that?'*
'No.'

◆ *'What would happen if you did that?'*
'I'm not sure.'

◆ *'Do you see any risks of that approach.'*
'No. I guess it might work.'

◆ *'Why do you think it would work?'*
'The clients wouldn't have to wait so long. And you would have more time to process their paperwork.'

◆ *'So what do you think?'*
'I think it sounds like a good idea.'

◆ *'Let's see how it goes.'*

Regardless of whether you are using formal training, coaching, or counselling, remember that the point is to make sure that volunteers learn from experience. The mix of methods which you choose may vary from volunteer to volunteer, and even will vary over the term of the volunteer's relationship with the organisation.

You can determine whether the learning experience has been a successful one by asking questions of the volunteer following the training. Some useful questions include:

◆ *What point sticks out in your mind?*

◆ *Why is that point so important?*

◆ *What did you hear that will be most useful to you?*

◆ *Why do you think so?*

◆ *How can you use this information in your volunteer job?*

◆ *What implication does this have for your ability to be successful here?*

Training as a volunteer benefit

Training might also be developed for the volunteer programme because it serves as a tangible benefit that could be offered to the volunteer in addition to the training required for satisfactory job performance.

The training might be developed by the organisation or might provide an opportunity for the volunteer to attend outside conferences or workshops. Attendance would be both an opportunity to increase knowledge and a formal recognition by the organisation that the volunteer is 'worth' the expense of sending on the training and confidence in them being an effective representative of the organisation.

With some volunteers, training can be a significant benefit. Young volunteers, for example, who came to volunteering as a means of gaining career experience might be offered sessions on volunteering as a step to paid employment, in CV writing, and in career planning.

Such training could be:

◆ Training in ancillary skills

◆ Training in career/life development

◆ Cause-related training

You should remember that training of any kind is almost always viewed with approval by volunteers. One of the primary benefits you can provide a volunteer is additional information, skills, or assistance in performing their work more productively, but you might also provide training in other areas of their life. Do not hesitate to ask for an additional commitment or effort from the volunteer in return for training, since most of them will regard it as well worth the effort. To the volunteer, your interest in them is regarded as a recognition of the significance and importance of their contribution to the work of the organisation.

Topics covered include:

- **Creating a motivating environment for your volunteers**

- **Managing people by asking questions, rather than by telling them what to do**

- **Evaluation and feedback**

- **Managing volunteers at a distance, professional volunteers and volunteers volunteering as a group**

- **Firing a volunteer – and the alternative**

This chapter identifies the techniques needed to manage your volunteer supervision effectively. And what to do if it all goes wrong.

EMPOWERING VOLUNTEERS

The effective volunteer manager needs skills in managing people for two reasons. First, you may be supervising volunteers who work for you directly in helping manage the volunteer programme. In addition, you must make sure that staff do a good job of managing the volunteers they are working with. Both of these areas demand knowledge of managing the relationship between volunteers and those they are working with and are responsible to. The most important element in this is the degree to which volunteers are empowered to make decisions regarding their work.

Being a manager of others

The manager's job is not to do things directly but to make sure things get done. Or to put it another way, the manager's job is to do things that enable others to do the work.

In order to succeed in this job, managers must learn to work indirectly, through other people. Most people who become volunteer managers are more used to doing things themselves. As you will see shortly, the instincts that serve one well in getting work done oneself are often counterproductive when it comes to getting things done through others.

Creating a motivating environment

We succeed in volunteer management primarily by creating conditions that encourage volunteers to want to do the work. By building a job around the volunteer's needs for volunteering, as described previously, we begin by placing the volunteer in a job s/he wants to do. We tap the volunteer's need for achievement by making sure there are goals to achieve. In this chapter we will look at tapping another need, the volunteer's need to feel in control of what s/he does. We do this using several techniques that empower the volunteer.

By 'empowering' volunteers, we mean making them more autonomous, more capable of independent action. The wisdom of this approach is that it is easier to get good results from empowered people than from people who are dependent. We can do this by giving them authority to decide, within limits, how they will go about achieving the results for which they are responsible. In such a relationship, the manager becomes a source of help for the volunteer, rather than a controller or a goad. This not only feels better for the volunteer, but allows the manager to spend less time making decisions about the volunteer's work and more time to think strategically, to concentrate on grasping the opportunities that will never be seen if you are mired in the muck of day-to-day detail.

Levels of control

In giving people authority over the 'how' of their jobs, the danger is that there is a risk that they will do the wrong things. This danger is reduced by recognising the different degrees of authority volunteers can exercise in carrying out their responsibilities. The four levels of control described below define how much say the supervisor and the volunteer each have in deciding how each result is to be achieved.

❶ *Self-assignment*

Self-assignment means that volunteers generate their own assignments. At this first level, the volunteer decides what to do, does it, and that is the end of it. A person working as a tutor in a literacy programme, for example, might meet with a client at the client's home, conduct tutoring, and go home. Next week, s/he repeat this routine. If the person were operating at level one on the control scale, s/he would do this without bothering to inform the paid staff what s/he had done or the progress s/he had made with the client.

This type of complete volunteer control rightly sends shivers of anxiety up the spine of most managers. The supervisor has no insurance that the volunteer did the right things or indeed did anything at all. A lesser degree of control might therefore be more appropriate.

❷ *Monitoring progress*

Regular progress reports are made at this second level of control. The volunteer decides what to do and does it, but at some point (the frequency of which is determined by the supervisor) the volunteer tells the supervisor what they did (either orally or in writing). If the volunteer indeed did the wrong thing or did the right thing in the wrong way, the supervisor finds out about it and can take steps to sort matters out. This gives the supervisor a bit more assurance that things will all work out properly in the end.

The frequency of progress reports depends on how anxious the supervisor is about the volunteer's performance. In the above example, if the supervisor has great confidence in the volunteer, s/he might only check progress once a month, finding out how the tutoring had gone, what the client had learned, what problems were encountered, how these were handled and what materials were needed. Moderate anxiety might require a report after each session. A higher degree of anxiety might warrant giving the volunteer a lesser degree of control.

❸ *Prior approval*

If the supervisor is very anxious about the volunteer's performance and is worried about having to 'fix it' more often than desirable, one option might be for volunteers to state beforehand what they intend to do. When volunteers operate at this third level of control, they are still the source of their own assignments. However, before taking action, their ideas are approved by the supervisor.

When a volunteer operates at this third level, the supervisor has pretty much complete assurance that the volunteer will do the right things. The supervisor has an effective veto over the volunteer.

Just as level two contains gradations of control in the form of varying frequencies of reports, level three comes in a variety of shades. In some cases, a volunteer might provide daily recommendations— *'I suggest I call these people now,'* for example. On the other hand, the recommendation may be longer term, such as *'here is my plan to raise the client's reading level.'* These gradations depend again on the supervisor's degree of anxiety about the volunteer's performance in pursuing particular targets.

At this third level, as with level two, volunteers should provide regular progress reports. At level three, a progress report should also contain a plan for future action.

❹ *No Control*

If the supervisor's degree of anxiety about a volunteer's performance is extremely high, s/he might be tempted to allow still less control. The only step lower is essentially no control at all. At this level of control, it doesn't matter whether volunteers see what needs to be done. They just do what they are told.

At this level, the authority for deciding what the volunteer will do is transferred from the place where the work is actually done to the management level. This inevitably produces more work for the manager. The more people the manager supervises, the more time will have to be spent deciding what people should be doing.

Besides taking more time, this style of management reduces the number of creative ideas you get from volunteers. Good ideas for improving services will seldom surface if the volunteer is not expected to think. As the pace of change accelerates, yesterday's practices will become increasingly obsolete. Volunteers, partly because they are not submerged in the day-to-day details of running the organisation, can provide a valuable perspective on the changing environment and the innovations needed to stay relevant.

The only time you should supervise volunteers at this fourth level is when they are new to the work they do. When people first come on board, they usually don't know enough about the organisation or the work they will be doing to make an intelligent recommendation. Usually, the volunteer knows this very well and wants to be told what to do. For this reason, short-term volunteers are appropriately managed in this way. If the volunteer sticks around for a while, however, you run great risks to volunteer morale if you continue to deny them the authority to think for themselves.

Climbing the control ladder

The four levels of control are a ladder for people to climb. When a volunteer learns enough about the job to give an intelligent recommendation, they can be moved to level three.

As the volunteer progresses up the control scale, the amount of time you have to spend managing them decreases. Level four people take the most time because we have to do all the thinking, tell them what to do, and then check their progress. Level three people take less time because they do the thinking, they tell you what they intend to do, and then you check the progress. At level two, you simply check the progress.

Of course the ultimate in time savings is level one, where you don't even have to check the progress. This level has many dangers associated with it, however. One is that the volunteer may feel that you aren't interested in their work and may feel devalued and drop out. Another is that the volunteers may come to feel unconnected to the programme and lose the sense of belonging that is so important to so many people. And of course, there is always the possibility that even the most trusted and proven volunteer might create a disaster that at level one strikes without warning.

Many managers see only two of these four levels of control, and they see the wrong two. For many, the only alternative to telling people what to do is to turn them loose. At level four you will reap resentment, but at level one you risk chaos. Most volunteers should work at either level three or level two on most of their results.

Checkpoints

One of the most common management mistakes is failure to check progress. Unless the volunteer is at level one, the supervisor should keep track of what the volunteer has been doing. Even where the two parties have discussed in advance what was to be done, it is best to check regularly to ensure the volunteer is making progress toward the target than to wait until the end to be surprised that the result was different from what you expected.

A calendar, on which meetings or telephone conversations are scheduled is the easiest, cheapest, and one of the most effective of all management controls. By requiring regular progress reports, you gain three important advantages, not the least of which is that it lets people know that you are serious about their achievement of results.

Progress reports also help avoid crises and poor quality last minute work. This is particularly important on long-term projects where volunteers are expected to be 'self-starters.' Most human beings start each day asking themselves *What is the most urgent task I have to do today?'* If the volunteer project is not due for six months, it is easy to put off progress today. This will continue to happen until the due date is excruciatingly near. But if the volunteer knows s/he has to report progress tomorrow, s/he will regard the project with a greater sense of urgency today. By setting regular checkpoints, you ensure that volunteers make regular progress.

A further advantage of regular reports is that they enable the manager to spot problems while there is still a chance for corrective action. If the volunteer has misunderstood your intentions, for example, you can find this out early, before s/he has wasted a lot effort going in the wrong direction.

A common pitfall in reporting progress happens when volunteers provide their own assessment of what they did rather than telling you what they actually did. If the volunteer says *'Things went really well,'* this does not give the supervisor any information about what actually happened. When volunteers say things are 'fine,' they are saying things are going the way they pictured them going. The wise supervisor finds out if things are going the way s/he pictured them going.

MANAGING BY ASKING QUESTIONS

To get the best results, a good manager will ask a lot of questions. Questions enable the volunteer to feel involved leaving the questioner still very much in control.

Insecure, inexperienced supervisors think they should have all the answers. Whenever they interact with a volunteer, they feel that if they can't provide an answer to all the questions and have instant solutions for all the problems, they are failing. Such managers either make ill-considered decisions or make an excuse for a delay when presented with complex problems.

The root of this behaviour is the traditional manager's concern that the volunteers should have confidence in him or her. By contrast, an effective manager is most concerned that volunteers have confidence in themselves.

Volunteers who depend on their supervisor for all the answers do not grow on their own. Further, since such managers often think it is their job to tell their volunteers what to do and how to do it, they tend to foster volunteer apathy and resentment. Volunteers in such circumstances tend to stagnate and decay.

The process of management can be divided into sub-functions. Three of the most important are *planning, empowering,* and *evaluating.* For each function there are several key questions to ask.

❶ Planning questions

Planning refers to the manager's role in setting goals and making sure that the volunteer knows what to do. Planning is something managers should never do on their own; they should always involve the people who will be carrying out the plan. By involving the people

Some key planning questions to ask in formal, long-range planning sessions include:

- What is the purpose of our work?

- What obstacles do we face in achieving that purpose?

- What resources do we have available to help us achieve our purpose?

- What strategies can we employ to overcome our major obstacles?

- What new developments affect us?

- What are the trends?

- How can we take advantage of those developments and trends?

- If we were to start the project all over again from scratch, what would we do differently?

- What problems are looming?

- What opportunities are presenting themselves?

who will be responsible for implementing the plan, you will give them a sense of ownership of the plan. You also make sure that the plan is based on the practical realities your volunteers face day-to-day. And you increase the likelihood that people will pursue the plan with enthusiasm.

In groups larger than six or seven, the manager will find it easier to increase active participation by having small groups of volunteers meet to discuss these questions and then report their conclusions to the whole group. With the data generated in response to these questions, the manager brings the group to focus by using questions such as:

◆   *Based on all this, what should we be trying to accomplish?*

◆   *What should our goals be for the forthcoming period?*

In all this the manager should not play a purely facilitative role. They may have strong opinions of their own. The manager should always get the most out of the group first. You should question first, suggest second, and only third state your own opinion. The idea is to encourage the volunteers to take ownership of the ideas, but to stay in control and ensure that effective goals are set for the organisation.

At this point, however, no one in particular has responsibility for any specific goal. One very powerful next move is to refer to each goal and ask the question *'Who will take responsibility for achieving this goal?'* Again, the manager may have particular people in mind, and can certainly exercise his or her prerogative to assign responsibility. But where it is appropriate, asking for voluntary assumption of responsibility leads to more committed pursuit of the organisation's objectives.

Other planning questions are appropriate after goals have been set and responsibility has been assigned or taken. At meetings with the responsible individual or team, these questions can be asked:

◆   *When can you have your plan for achieving these goals to me?*

◆   *When can you have this finished?*

◆   *How will you measure your success?*

◆   *What is your timetable?*

Questions can also be used to encourage volunteers to set short term goals for themselves and to maintain a sense of purpose on a daily basis. Two powerful questions in this regard include:

◆   *What do you intend to accomplish this month?*

◆   *What can you do today to progress toward your goals?*

◆   *What can you do today that will make the most difference?*

❷ Empowering questions

This second group of questions can be used in counselling and coaching volunteers on job performance and motivational issues. They include

- *How do you feel about your job?*
- *What are your frustrations?*
- *Do you know what you want to achieve in your job? What do you need to do your job better?*
- *Would you like some increased responsibility?*
- *Is there something you would rather do than what you do here now?*

When volunteers encounter difficulties or setbacks, they tend to get discouraged and may drop out. They tend to focus on what they can't control, namely their past action, and begin to feel frustrated and helpless. To avoid this, you need to keep them from focusing on what they did in the past and focus them on what they will do differently in the future. The main question you should ask about the past difficulty is:

- *What can you learn from this to help you in the future?*

You might then want to probe a bit asking questions such as:

- *What is your analysis of why this problem exists?*
- *What alternatives do you see?*
- *What are their strengths and weaknesses ?*
- *Is there a more productive way to look at this situation?*

But you quickly want to direct them to future action, to the things they can control. Questions to focus volunteers on future action include:

- *What is your recommendation?*
- *What can you do to get back on target?*
- *What one small step will start to make this situation better?*
- *What do you wish would happen?*
- *What could you do to make those wishes a reality?*
- *How could you get closer to the desired situation than you are today?*

❸ Evaluation questions

The third group of questions attempt to evaluate the effectiveness of the volunteer's performance. Questions that help do this include:

♦ *How would you evaluate your performance?*

♦ *Are you on-target or off?*

♦ *What went wrong?*

♦ *Why did you do it so well?*

♦ *What are some better ways of doing what you do?*

These questions ask the volunteers to evaluate their own performance and the reasons for it. They encourage the volunteers to do a self-assessment and take their own corrective action.

EFFECTIVE DELEGATION

One of the primary responsibilities of the manager is to delegate responsibility. In a volunteer management system, delegation can occur in a number of formats: volunteer manager to volunteers; project staff to volunteers; and volunteers to volunteers.

When delegating tasks to volunteers, the following elements ought to be included :

❶ Define the assignment in terms of results

Delegation is the art of giving a person the authority to carry out a mutually agreed task. The most fundamental skill involved is defining the task. This should be phrased in terms of an outcome or something to accomplish. It should define the desired end-product, not the means of achieving it.

For example, imagine that one of the tasks on your list of things to do today is to visit an electronics fair to see if

---

QUESTIONS FOR YOURSELF

Being a manager means being concerned about the ability of your people to fulfil their responsibilities to the organisation and its clients. Some questions to ask yourself from time to time to make sure you are paying attention to your management responsibilities include:

♦ *Do my volunteers know what they're supposed to accomplish?*

♦ *Do they have sufficient authority to accomplish it?*

♦ *Do I and they know if they are succeeding or not?*

♦ *Do they have the skills and knowledge necessary to succeed?*

♦ *Are things organised so that their responsibilities are clear?*

♦ *How long has it been since I gave each of them any recognition for their contributions and achievements?*

If you get negative answers to the first five of these questions, it means you have probably been spending too much time doing things yourself and not enough time managing. If your volunteers don't know what they are supposed to accomplish, for example, you have some goal-setting to do. If they lack skills, you have some training to do. And so on. If your answer to the last question is more than two weeks, you should make a special effort to let volunteers know that they are appreciated.

there is any new equipment your organisation might profit from. Instead of telling the volunteer to go to the exhibition to see what new equipment is available, you could delegate the desired outcome of the activity. You might say something like *'I would like to give you the responsibility for upgrading our equipment'*, or *'I wonder if you would be willing to take the responsibility for improving our efficiency through the purchase of new equipment'*.

Delegating by telling someone to go to the electronics fair removes one task from your list of things to do. Delegating by defining the result you want to achieve also removes all the tasks related to that result from all future days' lists.

❷ Define the level of control

The second step in delegating effectively is to define how much authority the person has in carrying out the responsibility. This involves choosing among four levels of control described earlier in this chapter. Keep as much authority for deciding how to do the work in the hands of the worker.

To continue the example above, you might say *'I would like to see your plan for doing this before you get started'*, thereby placing the volunteer at level three. *'Let's get together every Friday for a chat about your progress on this'*, puts the volunteer at level two.

❸ Communicate any guidelines

If there are relevant policies, laws, or regulations that the volunteer should work within, it is important to communicate these clearly at the outset.

To continue our example, the organisation may have purchasing regulations that need to be adhered to, such as getting price quotations from at least three suppliers. The volunteer needs to know this before wasting a lot of time doing something that would fall outside the rules.

❹ Make resources available

If you know of any resources that would make the job easier or increase the chance of success, you should mention these at the outset. Resources include people, manuals, events, institutions, and equipment that would be helpful in achieving the result. It also includes the budget, if any, for the task. At this point, you should stress that if the volunteer encounters difficulty, s/he must come to you for advice. When giving advice, however, it is important to make sure that you keep the authority for the work in the hands of the worker, that, if at all possible, you avoid telling the worker what to do.

In our example, you would want to tell the volunteer that the electronics fair is there. You would also refer them to any staff with expertise in this area. And above all, you would tell them how much money was available for the project. *'Don't waste your time looking at anything that costs more than £1000'*, for example.

❺ Determine criteria for success

The volunteer should know, at the outset, how his or her work will be judged. S/he should be involved in determining the criteria, and should have access to the data that indicates success or failure as s/he attempts to fulfil the responsibility.

In our example, you might say that the organisation wants a piece of equipment that will pay for itself in a year's time.

❻ Set up checkpoints

Unless the volunteer is at level one on the control scale, s/he should note on a calendar when s/he will be expected to report progress to you. The frequency of these checkpoints depends on your anxiety about the volunteer fulfilling the particular responsibility. These should not be presented to the volunteer as an excessively formal review meeting. Rather, it is an informal chat so you can find out how things are proceeding.

MAINTAINING COMMUNICATION

It is desirable to establish a system for providing on-going supervisory support for the volunteer. There are two main elements necessary for this.

Availability

Supervisors must be available to volunteers. The volunteers must have the ability to meet with, report to, and talk with supervisors, both on a regularly scheduled basis (checkpoints) and at times of the volunteer's choosing.

If the supervisor is available to the volunteer, the volunteer will feel that their work is appreciated enough to merit the attention and time of the supervisor. Availability also encourages the volunteer to consult with the supervisor when and if difficulties are encountered.

Supervisors can schedule time during office hours when volunteers can make appointments. Specific lunch meetings for groups of volunteers can be scheduled for open discussions. Supervisors can practice 'management by walking around' so that they can be approached by volunteers. Greeting volunteers

> " If the supervisor is available to the volunteer, the volunteer will feel that their work is appreciated enough to merit the attention and time of the supervisor. "

when they arrive for work and thanking them when they leave also provides the volunteer with a sense of access. The intent of all these methods is to develop a sense of open and ready communication and access.

Equal status and involvement

The second key element necessary to on-going supervisory support is a sense among the volunteers that they are being accorded equal status and involvement in the work of the organisation.

This equal treatment includes participation in decision-making (being invited to meetings or being asked for opinions, for example) and participation in day-to-day activities of the organisation (being on memo distribution lists, for example). To provide volunteers with a sense of being full partners in the organisation, they should be entitled to most of the same benefits that staff are entitled, such as access to training and trips, reimbursement of expenses, and proper job titles.

Perhaps the most challenging aspect of all of this is getting staff to remember volunteer names. People often forget the name of a volunteer who they rarely work with. When they see the volunteer, they say hello, but don't remember their name. One way to reduce this problem is to put pictures of volunteers and staff on a bulletin board or in a who's who directory so people can refresh their memories.

Volunteers get a sense of being second-class citizens when they perceive that they are excluded from staff activities and benefits. These exclusions are often subtle, such as reserved parking for staff but not for volunteers, or no one ever thinking to invite volunteers to staff meetings. When volunteers feel they are 'less' than staff, their self-esteem suffers, and they may stop wanting to volunteer.

Perhaps the most important aspect of building a sense of equality is open and free communication. This includes adding them to the newsletter mailing lists, making sure they are copied on correspondence that involves their work, or taking the time to update a volunteer on what has happened since s/he was last there.

EVALUATION AND FEEDBACK

Volunteer managers should develop a process for providing evaluation and feedback to volunteers. While often viewed negatively by those who have to administer it, a good evaluation process is actually of value to those who are judged by it, since it

provides them with feedback necessary to determine how well they are doing and to obtain suggestions on how to improve their performance. Regular evaluation sessions with volunteers are desirable both to help the volunteer work closer to their potential, and to help the organisation better utilise volunteers. Evaluation sessions should not deal with all the small performance problems that supervisors have been ignoring since the last evaluation session. This would distract from their main function, which is not day-to-day management.

Regular, scheduled feedback

Volunteers should receive feedback at regular intervals. The interval should be more frequent when the volunteer first starts (monthly for the first six months) and then should be biannual. The benefit of this regular scheduling for formal feedback is that it forces the supervisor to let the volunteer know how s/he is doing and how to improve. Too often, this feedback is put off by busy supervisors. In the absence of regular scheduling, performance issues tend to be avoided until minor difficulties turn into major problems.

A system established for providing this feedback would include the following steps:

- Have a policy on performance appraisal and review
- Apply the policy to both volunteers and staff
- Develop performance criteria with each volunteer
- Explain expectations and procedures in advance

One method for creating this system is simply to adapt the evaluation system in place for paid staff, assuming, naturally, that there is already an evaluation system for paid staff in operation.

TIPS FOR IMPLEMENTING THE VOLUNTEER EVALUATION SYSTEM:

- **Don't get overwhelmed by forms:**
  the substance is more important than the paperwork.

- **Start with the job description:**
  it should provide a groundwork for discussing what the volunteer has been doing, and if it doesn't it should be rewritten.

- **Stick to the basics:**
  job proficiency, working relationships, comparison with last review.

- **Listen at least as much as you talk:**
  one way to look at the evaluation session is as a 'follow-up' volunteer interview, allowing you to see whether the needs and interests of the volunteer have changed enough to require a new assignment.

- **Evaluation:**
  Remember it may show as much what *you* need to do as it does what the volunteer needs to do.

The positive side of evaluation

Rather than thinking of evaluation as a system for dealing with problems, you ought to think of it as a means of rewarding those who are doing well. The percentage of volunteers who are troublesome is fairly small; those who are hard-working constitute the vast majority. This means that the majority of evaluation comments can be positive ones, praising the work that is being accomplished.

The evaluation session can also be diagnostic in nature, allowing you to determine how volunteers are feeling about their work. For example, volunteers who are in intensive job positions (such as providing advocacy for abused children) often get 'burned out.' Volunteers also frequently fail to recognise such problems and fail to ask for help, since their commitment drives them to continue to work. The evaluation session can provide the astute volunteer manager with the opportunity to determine whether a good volunteer is becoming burned out, or bored, or needing to be transferred to another position. You can also find out a volunteer's readiness to be promoted to increased responsibility. The session thus becomes one of mutual evaluation, with the intent of rewarding and advancing those who have been productive.

SPECIAL CASES

There are several special situations which require particular care in supervision. Here are five examples which require some adaptation of the general principles:

❶ The assigned volunteer

An increasingly common situation involves the volunteer who is assigned to work directly with a particular member of staff rather than being under the immediate control of the volunteer manager.

The staff to whom the volunteer is assigned may neglect basic volunteer management functions, leaving the volunteer with a feeling of being stranded without any support system. Some staff may engage in 'benign neglect,' appreciating whatever work they obtain from the volunteer, but not viewing them as they would a paid employee doing an equivalent job to whom they would feel some supervisory responsibility. Some staff may engage in sporadic supervision, paying close attention to specific work assignments, but avoiding what they may view as 'less important' aspects of supervision, such as periodic evaluations.

If specific volunteers are going to be working exclusively with a single member of staff, then it is essential to convey to that person

THE ASSIGNED VOLUNTEER

The key to avoiding problems with assigned volunteers is for the volunteer manager to reach a clear understanding with those staff who are assigned volunteers over who performs what aspects of supervision and management of the volunteer. Areas of confusion include:

♦ Who completes a job description for the volunteer and who periodically reviews and updates it?

♦ Who interviews potential candidates for the position?

♦ Who accepts the volunteer for the position?

♦ Who completes necessary paperwork and personnel forms?

♦ Who is responsible for on-the-job training of the volunteer?

♦ Who will be responsible for providing work assignments for the volunteer or for contacting the volunteer to inform them that no work is available?

♦ Who will ensure that the volunteer is kept in touch with information and decisions relevant to his or her work?

♦ Who will ensure that the volunteer has a work space and equipment?

♦ Who will be available to talk to the volunteer if there is a problem with work or scheduling?

♦ Who will evaluate the volunteer?

♦ Who has the authority and responsibility to correct the volunteer's behaviour if there are problems, or to terminate the relationship?

♦ Who is responsible for the volunteer when the designated staff person is absent?

that they must act as the 'supervisor' of the volunteer, and must provide a link to the organisation and its work. This means that the member of staff must accept responsibility for ensuring that the volunteer is provided with work and working conditions that enable the volunteer to both be and feel successful.

❷ The floating volunteer

Occasionally, volunteers may be assigned to various parts of the organisation on a temporary basis, working today with one group of staff and tomorrow with another. While these volunteers will, over time, develop their own linkages with individual members of staff, it is recommended that the volunteer manager assume responsibility for most of the supervision of these 'floating' volunteers.

Staff to whom the volunteer is temporarily assigned can provide supervision over direct job functions. They will be unable to do more than this.

To avoid problems, the volunteer manager should take responsibility for the following:

◆ Act as the official 'greeter' to the volunteer when they arrive at the organisation, and receive the volunteer at the beginning of each new work assignment and escort them to their new worksite to introduce them to the new staff with whom they will be working.

◆ Serve as an on-going social and communication link between the volunteer and the organisation. This will mean making sure that the volunteer receives updates on organisation policy and decisions relevant to their volunteer job. It might also mean creating a small social group of other floating volunteers who meet periodically to keep in touch.

◆ Provide on-going evaluation discussions, based on information gathered from staff with whom the volunteer has worked, and continuing to strive to find volunteer assignments that will meet the volunteer's changing talents and needs.

❸ Long distance volunteers

The long-distance or 'invisible' volunteer, who works in the field without day-to-day contact with the organisation and who may never even have been to the organisation's office requires a different approach.

There are two challenges. The first is communicating with them, *(see table overleaf)* and the second involves making sure they are doing the right things. These issues of communication and control require special efforts on the part of the supervisor. Regularly scheduled weekly phone calls and sending regular information (newsletters, memo's etc.) help to keep the long distance volunteer informed and feeling part of the organisation. You can even ask the volunteer to contribute occasionally to your newsletter.

Controlling long distance volunteers

The second challenge can be met by setting clear goals for the volunteer, as described in the chapter on job design, and asking for frequent progress reports. To keep the volunteer feeling

COMMUNICATING WITH LONG DISTANCE VOLUNTEERS

Here are some general tips for communicating with long distance volunteers:

◆ Volunteers in isolated or separated settings will naturally have more communication problems than those who are gathered in one spot. The smart supervisor will simply plan for this difficulty and adjust to compensate. Generally speaking, things will take longer, will have a greater chance of being misunderstood, and will need to be managed more carefully.

◆ Volunteers in isolated or separated settings are prone to develop fears about their exclusion from the system. They will worry about whether they are being kept properly informed of things (whilst decisions are being considered and after they have been made) and whether their input is sought and valued.

◆ Withholding information from your people creates a sense of second class status. People from whom information is withheld will go to extraordinary lengths to either obtain the information or to create their own versions of what is going on.

◆ When decisions that affect particular people are being made, every effort should be made to involve those people in the decision-making process. Bringing people together for discussion is the best way to accomplish this. Technology can supplement but not totally replace face-to-face communication.

◆ Strive to achieve a sense of 'personal' contact between headquarters and the field. People are more likely to communicate with those that they 'know' and are often more likely to forgive errors in communication. Bringing volunteers to visit headquarters is one way to begin accomplishing this. Publishing a telephone directory with photographs is another.

◆ The longer it takes for a decision to be made at head office, the more left out people will feel. The more important the issue, the longer the response time will 'seem.' Strive to get back as quickly as possible, if only to deliver an interim response.

◆ Much communication takes place by osmosis − you learn things simply because you are in the vicinity of their occurrence. A supervisor at headquarters is in a much better position to learn via osmosis than a field volunteer. The smart supervisor proactively attempts to pass along as much information as possible to the field. It is better to pass more information than is needed than to give the field a sense that you are restricting their access to information.

◆ Good communication should be viewed as a 'web' connecting all within the system − it should function up, down, sideways and across. If you do not design your communication system to function this way, your volunteers will re-engineer it to do so, and will probably leave you out of their design.

◆ Uniformity should not be pursued as an end in itself. Use what works, which may be very different with volunteers in different situations.

bonded to the organisation, consider having social events in which long-distance volunteers get together with staff for sharing of 'war stories' and good fellowship.

The main tension between supervisors and long-distance volunteers is between the volunteer's need to decide what they will do and the supervisor's need to make sure that those things are done effectively. To minimise the conflict, do the following:

◆ Establish clear priorities to guide volunteer's daily decisions. These priorities should give volunteers a clear sense of what is important and how their time should be spent – even when a supervisor is not around to give immediate instructions.

◆ Ask volunteers to recommend measurable, attainable goals each month. These goals should relate to the established priorities.

◆ Have regularly scheduled chats to check the volunteer's progress toward those goals. Allocate your time and attention according to your experience with each volunteer. Direct more attention to those who have shown the need for monitoring or redirection, but do not ignore the good performers simply because they are not causing problems. If you ignore them they may eventually cause problems just to get your attention.

It would also be well to remember when dealing with long distance volunteers that it is the same entrepreneurial traits (an ability to work alone, an ability to make decisions and be self-initiating) that make a long distance volunteer successful which will also make that same volunteer difficult to 'control.' Supervisors may simply have to recognise that their ability to closely direct the work of those who work alone in the field has different limitations than lies with those who work more contiguously.

❹ Volunteer professionals

The fourth special case involves the supervision of volunteers who have professional credentials, and who are possessed of more expertise than the staff who are their supervisors. This imbalance in knowledge, experience, and sometimes even status may make it difficult for staff to feel comfortable in exercising 'control' over the professional, and may make it difficult for the professional to accept close supervision.

Step one in involving professionals as volunteers is job development. A common mistake is to assume that the professional should be the one who designs their own job, since they are the experts. While it is true that the professional can probably best determine how the work should be done, it is equally true that the other aspects of job design must be carried out with the involvement of the volunteer manager.

This includes determining the exact purpose of the job and the results that are desired. The professional will need to be told what is to be accomplished and why those results are important. Outlining these elements will serve both to better motivate the professional and to assist them in deciding how best to undertake the work. After all, the professional knows lots of 'answers'; the problem lies in figuring out which ones are correct for this particular situation. The more information you can give them about what you really need, the better they can match their knowledge to your specific concerns.

A further aspect involves setting the parameters of the job. This will include items such as desired timeframe for completion, available support system, treatment of expenses, and needs for reporting and approvals. All of these will need to be discussed and negotiated with the professional volunteer, many of whom will be accustomed to exercising virtual autonomy and independent control over their work.

While this independence on their part works well for them, you may find it uncomfortable. A common problem is that their notion of expenses may not match your capacities. A lawyer may incur several hundred pounds worth of quite reasonable expenses in an afternoon, and be accustomed to billing these to clients. You, on the other hand, might find that amount to be larger than the entire budget for your project...

Another common problem lies in setting out what matters require approval. If, for example, plans need to be approved by the management committee before they can be implemented, then this should be explained at the start.

In practice, more time needs to be spent on job design and negotiation with volunteer professionals than with most other categories of volunteers. Because the professionals are more likely to work independently and be self-supervising, it is imperative to have a clear initial mutual understanding of the desired results, parameters, and process of the volunteer work.

Supervision of the professional volunteer may assume some different forms. If you are working with large numbers of professionals, then it is sometimes very helpful to recruit a lead volunteer from the group, who will act as your intermediary, assuming responsibility for supervision. This peer relationship will make it easier for them to deal with any problem situations.

For situations in which only one professional is recruited, then sometimes a quasi-buddy system works well. One person (sometimes a member of staff and sometimes a volunteer) is appointed to 'work with' the professional, operating as primary liaison with the organisation. This person both monitors the progress of the work and helps the professional by retrieving information from the organisation, presenting reports, etc. This 'informal supervision' allows you to maintain some control of the situation without risking ego problems.

A common problem encountered in supervising expert professionals lies in 'back seat driving'. You have recruited them for their expertise: they know how to solve the problem and you don't. This means that you must trust that expertise, which is often more difficult than it sounds.

> Marlene Wilson relates a wonderful story of recruiting an advertising expert to help design a new brochure for an organisation. The expert was internationally acclaimed for her work, had agreed to help out, and eventually presented her suggested design. Marlene, who like most of us has her own preferences in style, started to make a few 'suggestions.' The expert stopped her, and asked 'Why did you ask me to do this job, Marlene?' . After a moment she realised that it was because she was, in fact, *the expert*, which meant she might well keep her opinions to herself. The brochure, unchanged, went on to win several design awards.

The volunteer professional may, in truth, have a much better notion of how well the job is progressing than you do, and any evaluation of the work may rely on their expertise. If the contribution of the professional is to be on-going or on an annual basis, then you might want to conduct an evaluation or debriefing session, and review the work or project much like you would a special event, concentrating on how can you do this better in the future.

❺ Groups of volunteers

A volunteer manager may occasionally involve as a volunteer unit a group of people, such as a club. This group will have its own identity, its own structure, and will view itself as volunteering as a group rather than as individuals. Keeping supervisory control over the actions of group volunteers can be a tricky job, as you have to keep a balance between the volunteers feeling ownership and responsibility and having your organisation in control over what is done in its name. Consider the following as ways to juggle the two needs:

◆ When events or activities are to be done by group volunteers, offer clear, simple guidelines in a step-by-step fashion. Make sure the mission of the effort is clearly outlined. If there are any restrictions or requirements that need to be explained, let people know quickly. An example of this might be any restriction on the use of the organisation's name or logo or any requirement for crediting or not crediting corporate sponsorship. You don't want to wake up one morning and discover you're operating the IBM Food Bank Marathon because the group itself has gone out and got that support.

◆ If the project or activity has been done before, give the group all the information you have about what was done, what worked, and what didn't.

◆ Be clear about the various jobs that need to be done. For complex efforts, provide sample job descriptions and indicate how the jobs interconnect and work together toward the common goal.

◆ Clearly outline supervisory responsibility between you, the group, and its individual members. Make sure everyone is in agreement about who is in charge of what and of whom.

◆ Establish reporting dates and a channel for communication between you and the group. Meet more frequently early in the relationship so you can identify any problems or confusions and be helpful.

◆ Get the group to appoint its own 'volunteer manager' with whom you will work. This is especially important for a one-shot event, such as a weekend construction project. Work with this person to help them with recruitment, on-the-job supervision, and overall management. *Make sure that someone understands that they are in charge of overseeing the project.*

FIRING A VOLUNTEER

One of the recurrent nightmares of any volunteer manager is encountering a situation where they may have to consider 'firing' a volunteer. For many, this prospect creates severe stress, both over the appropriateness of the action and over fear of possible legal and political consequences.

This section is intended to provide some guidelines on developing a system that will assist both in confronting the problem and in managing the decision to terminate a volunteer's relationship with the organisation.

Getting philosophically ready

The initial requirement in developing a system for handling volunteer termination is to decide that firing volunteers is, in the appropriate circumstances, a necessary action. This is often a difficult step for many volunteer managers, probably because they are very people-oriented and respect the willingness of others to help. There is particular difficulty in dealing with situations where the decision to terminate is not due to any particular 'fault' on the part of the volunteer, but is instead due to ill health or a change in programme needs. Where there has been a focus on volunteering as a benefit to the volunteer (such as some retirement volunteering programmes) managers may also have great difficulty with this because they classify volunteers as 'clients', and it is philosophically difficult to justify terminating a client.

> **Ann Cook, in a survey of Foster Grandparents Programmes in 23 communities found that 82% of responding volunteer managers rated the decision to terminate a volunteer as being a 'difficult or very difficult issue' for them. Over 60% of the volunteer managers reported delaying dealing with the problem.**

There are several rationales for firing volunteers. One is simply that the bottom line is the ability to deliver quality service to the clients of the organisation and any barrier to that delivery is not allowable. This standard would apply to both paid and unpaid staff, as Jane Mallory Park points out: *'Whether the personnel in question are paid or volunteer, it is important to have policies and practices which promote accountability and the highest levels of performance possible without ignoring the reality that all individuals have idiosyncrasies and limitations as well as strengths. A double standard which does not give respect and dignity to both volunteers and paid staff is not only unnecessary but is also unhealthy for individuals and organisations.'*

A second approach has to do with giving meaning and value to volunteer service. By denying that there is a 'right' and a 'wrong' way to do a volunteer job, one conveys the impression that the volunteer work done is irrelevant and insignificant. An organisation which does not care enough about the work done by volunteers to enforce quality communicates to other volunteers that the organisation believes their own work to be meaningless.

The philosophical decision by an organisation to fire volunteers is one that should be addressed before any need to do so arises. It should be discussed and ratified by staff and then codified as part of the overall policy statement on volunteer use and included as part of the organisation's volunteer policies.

Developing a system for making firing decisions

If you do encounter a situation where none of the alternatives *(see table on p112)* work, it is helpful to have in place a system for dealing with the problem. Some organisations have been sued by terminated volunteers (this possibility depends on whether the volunteer is deemed to have had a contract of employment under the employment protection legislation) and dismissal may cause

ALTERNATIVES TO FIRING

A decision to terminate a volunteer should always be, in practice, a reluctant last resort. Firing a volunteer is an admission that volunteer management has failed. It means that the interviewing system did not work, or the job design was faulty, or that training and supervision did not operate the way it should. It is as much an indictment of the manager as it is of the volunteer.

And it is crucial to remember that many situations that appear to warrant firing may actually be remediable by less stringent methods. Before contemplating firing a volunteer, see if any of the following approaches may be more appropriate and less painful:

♦ **Re-supervise**

You may have a volunteer who doesn't understand that rules have to be followed. This is a common problem with young volunteers, some of whom automatically 'test' the rules as part of their self-expression. Enforcement may end the problem.

♦ **Re-assign**

Transfer the volunteer to a new position. You may, on the basis of a short interview, have misread their skills or inclinations. They may simply not be getting along with the staff or other volunteers with whom they are working. Try them in a new setting and see what happens.

♦ **Re-train**

Send them back for a second education. Some people take longer than others to learn new techniques. Some may require a different training approach, such as one-on-one mentoring rather than classroom lectures. If the problem is lack of knowledge rather than lack of motivation, then work to provide the knowledge.

♦ **Re-vitalise**

If a longtime volunteer has started to malfunction, they may just need a rest. This is particularly true with volunteers who have intense jobs, such as one-to-one work with troubled clients. The volunteer may not realise or admit that they're burned out. Give them a sabbatical and let them recharge. Practice 'crop rotation' and transfer them temporarily to something that is less emotionally draining.

♦ **Refer**

Maybe they just need a whole new outlook of life, one they can only get by volunteering in an entirely different organisation. Refer them to the Volunteer Bureau or set up an exchange programme with a sister organisation. Swap your volunteers for a few months and let them learn a few new tricks.

♦ **Retire**

Recognise that some volunteers may no longer be able to do the work they once could and may even be a danger to themselves and to others. Give them the honour they deserve and ensure that they don't end their volunteer careers in a way they will regret. Assist them in departing with dignity before the situation becomes a tragic crisis.

All of these alternatives are both easier to implement and managerially smarter than making a decision to fire a volunteer. They recognise that there are many reasons why a person may be behaving inappropriately and that some of these reasons have answers other than dismissing that person. We strongly urge that you consider each of these alternatives before deciding to fire any volunteer.

political and community relations problems. The system we propose is designed to help the volunteer manager both in making and in justifying the decision to terminate a volunteer. Essentially, it has three parts:

❶ *Forewarning/notice*

The first stage of the system is developing clear policies and information about the prospect of firing volunteers. To do this, you need to develop the following:

◆ A set of official personnel policies regarding the employment of volunteers. It is especially important to have policies on probation, suspension, and termination.

◆ A system for informing volunteers, in advance, about these policies. Volunteer induction should discuss the policies and provide examples of requirements and of unacceptable behaviour.

◆ A mechanism for relating these policies to each volunteer job. This means having a job description for the volunteer which explains the requirements of the job, and has some measurable objectives for determining whether the work is being accomplished satisfactorily.

❷ *Investigation/determination*

The second part of the system involves developing a process for determining whether the volunteer has actually broken the rules. This implies having a fair investigator take the time to examine the situation and reach a decision that something has been done wrongly. You should never terminate a volunteer 'on the spot,' regardless of the infraction. 'Instant firing' doesn't allow you to determine whether there are extenuating circumstances. This is why a suspension policy is so important.

Essentially, in this part of the system the volunteer manager needs to establish a process for reviewing the performance of volunteers and recording problems. This should be done as part of the regular evaluation process for volunteers. Those volunteers whose performance is unsatisfactory are told of their deficiency, counselled on improving their work, and then re-evaluated. Failure to conform to the quality standard over time can then become grounds for termination. In cases where the unsatisfactory performance is substantial in nature (inappropriate relations with a client or breach of confidentiality) then what is needed is some 'proof' that the volunteer did in fact commit the wrong-doing. This might be testimony from other volunteers, staff, or the client.

During this part of the process the volunteer manager also

investigates whether any of the alternatives to firing would provide a more appropriate solution.

❸ *Application*

This final part of the system requires that the volunteer manager do a fair job of enforcing the system. It requires equal and fair application of the rules (no playing favourites), appropriate penalties (graduated to the severity of the offence) and, if possible, a review process, so that the decision does not look like a personal one.

You will note that the above three processes mirror the common personnel practices for paid staff. They are, in fact the same, as they should be, since evaluating either paid or unpaid staff should follow the same rules.

The advantages of this system are two-fold. First, they assist the volunteer manager in reaching the right decision, and in feeling comfortable about making that decision. The system is fair to both the volunteer and the organisation and tends to produce 'correct' answers. It also allows the volunteer manager to divert to a less drastic solution where appropriate.

Second, the system helps develop a case for firing that can be used to explain the decision to others, internally and externally. A side-effect of this system is that many problem volunteers decide voluntarily to resign rather than face the inevitable and seemingly inexorable conclusion of the dismissal process. Most people prefer not to sit in front of an oncoming train.

CONDUCTING THE FIRING MEETING

Regardless of how the decision to terminate is reached, someone has to convey that decision to the volunteer. Fortunately, most supervisory experiences with volunteers will be pleasant, and you will spend more time assisting dedicated volunteers to maximise their performance. It is good, however, to be prepared for the exception, since it is one of the responsibilities of the effective volunteer manager to protect the programme and the other volunteers by dealing quickly and conclusively with problem volunteers.

◆ **Conduct the meeting in a private setting**
This will preserve the dignity of the volunteer and perhaps of yourself.

◆ **Be quick, direct, and absolute**
Don't beat around the bush. It is quite embarrassing to have the volunteer show up for work the next day because they didn't get the hint. Practice the exact words you will use in telling the volunteer, and make sure they are unequivocal. Do not back down from them even if you want to preserve your image as a 'nice person.'

◆ **Announce, don't argue**
The purpose of the meeting is simply, and solely, to communicate to the volunteer that they are being separated from the organisation. This meeting is not to re-discuss and re-argue the decision, because, if you have followed the system, all the arguments will already have been heard. You should also avoid arguing to make sure you don't put your foot in your mouth while venting your feelings. Expect the volunteer to vent, but keep yourself quiet.

◆ **Don't attempt to counsel**
If counselling were an option, you would not be having this meeting. Face reality; at this point you are not the friend of this former volunteer, and any attempt to appear so is mis-guided.

◆ **Follow-up**
Follow-up the meeting with a letter to the volunteer re-iterating the decision and informing them of any departure details. Make sure you also follow-up with others. Inform staff and clients of the change in status, although you do not need to inform them of the reasons behind the change. In particular, make sure that clients with a long relationship with the volunteer are informed of the new volunteer to whom they are assigned.

CHAPTER EIGHT
RETENTION & RECOGNITION

Topics covered include:

- ◆ **Understanding why volunteers volunteer**
- ◆ **Giving your volunteers a sense of esteem**
- ◆ **Retention strategies for short-term volunteers**
- ◆ **Volunteer recognition**

Retaining your volunteers is the key to success. There is no point in being good at recruitment, if you cannot keep them. This chapter examines motivation and reward.

MOTIVATION

As has been emphasised throughout this book, volunteer programmes are fuelled by the motivation of the volunteers and the staff of the organisation. Problems of volunteer retention can usually be traced to problems of motivation.

A motivated volunteer is one who wants to do the job that needs to be done in the spirit and within the guidelines of the organisation. People behave in motivated ways when the work satisfies a need of theirs. Children, for example, are motivated to open birthday presents because doing so meets a psychological need. Starting here, you correctly see that volunteer motivation comes from inside the volunteer, stemming from a set of needs which are satisfied by doing things which are found to be productive.

When you encounter volunteers who are not behaving as you would like, you may label them 'unmotivated', but actually this is incorrect. A so-called unmotivated person is actually just as motivated as a motivated person. S/he too needs, wants, and desires something. However, for reasons you will explore in this chapter, those needs are met in counterproductive ways. They behave in this way, because doing so is more satisfying than the behaviour you would like them to choose. In other words, people behave the way they do for a particular reason.

All behaviour is motivated

Sometimes, 'unmotivated' behaviour is caused by frustration. If a volunteer has a high need for achievement, for example, and sees little to accomplish or 'win' in the job, s/he may choose to set up a win-lose situation with those in authority. For example, a volunteer might go to the trustees every time there was a disagreement with staff, seeking to get the decision overturned. This so-called 'unmotivated' behaviour met the volunteer's need for achievement. It provided a challenge. It gave an opportunity to win.

When we talk about motivating volunteers, we are talking about creating a volunteer experience which allows an individual to meet his or her motivational needs in ways that are productive for the organisation and satisfying for the individual. You remove barriers to motivation by designing satisfying work experiences and create systems that allow volunteers to meet their needs. You make sure, in other words, that volunteers receive their motivational paycheck for the valuable contributions made to the work of the organisation. This is the essence of volunteer retention.

Because each volunteer has a different combination of needs, each will do best in different work conditions. One volunteer may be highly motivated by gaining job experience, whereas another may be highly motivated by the desire to meet new people, and a third may have a burning passion to do something to contribute to the cause. For the first, you need to make sure that the volunteer has the opportunity to learn the skills s/he wants to learn. The second must be placed in a work setting where s/he can work with others. The third needs a job that s/he sees making a meaningful contribution to the organisation's mission.

This is further complicated by the fact that a volunteer's needs may change over time. For example, a female volunteer may work well on an independent project. It satisfies her need to achieve something meaningful. Then her husband dies. Her need to be with others may suddenly become much more important than the need to achieve something meaningful. To satisfy this need and retain the volunteer, you might transfer her to a group project.

RETAINING VOLUNTEERS

The key to retaining volunteers is to make sure they are getting their particular complex of motivational needs (see table p117) met through their volunteer experience. When this is occurring across the volunteer programme, a positive, enthusiastic climate is created which, in turn, encourages people to continue to volunteer.

Creating an esteem-producing climate

Particularly effective for volunteer retention is what you call an

> "When we talk about motivating volunteers, we are talking about creating a volunteer experience which allows an individual to meet his or her motivational needs in ways that are productive for the organisation and satisfying for the individual. You remove barriers to motivation by designing satisfying work experiences and create systems that allow volunteers to meet their needs."

TO EACH THEIR OWN MIX

Volunteers have combinations of needs. The art of motivating volunteers lies not only in knowing how to tap a given motivator, but in being able to figure out what combination of needs a particular volunteer has. One way to do that is to ask the volunteers periodically. Discuss their rating of the relative importance of the following factors:

◆ To gain knowledge of community problems

◆ To maintain skills no longer used otherwise

◆ To spend 'quality time' with members of the family by volunteering together.

◆ To get out of the house.

◆ To make new friends.

◆ To be with old friends who volunteer here.

◆ To gain new skills.

◆ To have fun.

◆ To meet a challenge.

◆ To improve my community.

◆ To work with a certain client group.

◆ To be in charge of something.

◆ To be part of a group or a team.

◆ To gain work experience to help get a job.

◆ To meet important people in the community.

◆ To gain status with my employer.

◆ To get community recognition.

The mix of responses from the volunteers will give you a better feeling for why they want to volunteer and what you need to give them in return as their 'motivational paycheck'. For example, if a volunteer ranks the last three above as his or her highest needs, you will need to make sure they have a job which does indeed enable them to meet important people and which is highly visible in the community. To make sure that the employer is aware of the contribution, you can send a letter of commendation for his or her contribution.

esteem-producing climate. When the work environment boosts a person's self esteem, s/he feels good about her job, be it paid or volunteer work. S/he looks forward to going to the workplace.

Psychologists Harris Clams and Reynold Bean have studied self-esteem for many years. They found that people with high self-esteem are people who simultaneously satisfy three particular motivational needs. They enjoy a sense of *connectedness*, a sense of *uniqueness*, and a sense of *power* or *effectiveness*.

Connectedness

When people feel connected, they feel a sense of belonging, a sense of being part of a relationship with others. In a highly mobile society, where friends and loved ones may live hundreds of miles away and the next door neighbour is sometimes a stranger, this need is often unmet, leaving people with a sense of isolation, dissatisfaction, and loneliness. The psychologist William Glasser points out that this need is often stronger even than the need to survive, in that most people who try to commit suicide do so out of loneliness.

> **The following factors are most often mentioned as producing a sense of belonging:**
>
> - A common goal
> - Common values
> - Mutual respect
> - Mutual trust
> - A sense that one group member's weaknesses are made up for by another group member's strengths.

A sense of identification with a work group can meet this need, producing healthier, happier individuals. In our seminars over the past four years, we have surveyed more than 1,500 individuals who at one time in their lives felt a positive sense of connectedness.

People with a sense of connectedness have a sense of 'we' as well as a sense of 'I.' The more special the 'we' is, the more special the individual feels as part of the group and the greater the self-esteem that is generated. This is why it is important to have high standards for becoming a group member.

Leaders of volunteer programmes should be on the look out for comments people make about the expectations they have of themselves and their co-workers. If people say things like *'I'm just a volunteer,'* or *'What do they expect for free?'* it should cause alarm bells to ring. People's self-esteem drops when they regard themselves as part of a below average group. This negative sense of connectedness leads to high turnover of staff and volunteers. When they hear negative statements such as this, leaders should try to generate positive ideas for improving the connectedness situation. They might ask: *'What makes you say that? What can you do to improve this situation? What kind of place would you want to work? What can you do to make this organisation more like the kind of place you want it to be?'*

Positive feelings of connectedness can be enhanced in many ways, some of which have been referred to previously:

1 The volunteer manager can work with staff to make sure that there is a common purpose or goal for the team. Nothing is as fundamental to a team being effective as a common sense of what they are trying to achieve together. Both staff and volunteers should see themselves as equal partners in pursuing this goal.

2 In developing jobs for volunteers (other than for one-shot volunteers who you don't expect to retain), staff should avoid setting performance standards that are too low. If the expectations are too easy to meet, people will not feel special about their participation. Volunteers should not have lower standards than paid staff.

3 The volunteer manager should insure that staff and volunteers are treated equally. The volunteer manager should be on the lookout for inadvertent behaviour which makes volunteers feel excluded. A common example is that volunteers are not invited to staff meetings, not because they are deliberately excluded but because no one thought to give them the option to attend. Such a situation can make volunteers feel like second-class citizens.

4 When working with staff to develop jobs for volunteers, the volunteer manager should make sure that volunteers (or teams of volunteers) have a sense of ownership of a client or project. Fragmentation of ownership generates blame and criticism – which is the enemy of connectedness.

5 The volunteer manager should encourage leaders to celebrate the accomplishments of volunteers in the context of their contribution to the goals of the group. Recognition must be consistent so that people do not suspect favouritism. Team accomplishments can also be celebrated, giving equal credit to all team members.

Leaders should spread the word about positive accomplishments. They should talk about the values and standards of the organisation and what it means to be part of the group.

Leaders should look for opportunities to promote interaction among group members. This is particularly important where there are few 'natural' opportunities for people to share their common experiences. For example, in befriending schemes and literacy programmes, volunteers will be working with the client and in their own schedule. Volunteers work with little daily supervision and rarely appear in the office. Effective volunteer supervisors, knowing that *'it's lonely out there,'* take pains to bring their people together for training, pot lucks, and sharing of 'war stories.'

Another way to promote interaction is to involve people in the decision-making process. When each group member feels s/he has a say in deciding the unit's strategy, his/her feeling of connectedness is enhanced. In such meetings, it is important that you do not let your own biases and positions be known in advance. Group members who know what the person in authority wants will tend to support that position. If you already know the way you want to go, you might as well just tell them.

People's sense of connectedness is enhanced by engaging in new experiences together. By insisting passionately on constant improvement, leaders encourage people to try out new ways of doing things. If these are done by teams, the sense of connectedness grows.

Uniqueness

A second characteristic of people with high self-esteem is a feeling of uniqueness, a feeling that *'there is no one in the world quite like me.'* This means that I have a sense that I am special in some way, that I have a unique combination of talents or personal qualities.

Volunteer managers build feelings of uniqueness by recognising the achievements of individual group members and by praising them for their individual qualities. They encourage individuals to express themselves and, by giving them the authority to think, explore alternative ways to achieve their results.

People's uniqueness can also be enhanced by giving them challenging assignments that take advantage of their individual strengths. *'This is a difficult responsibility requiring your special talents,'* a volunteer's supervisor might say. Such a statement, of course, should be their sincere belief.

This need to feel unique is sometimes in conflict with a person's need to feel connected. All of us tend to make compromises in our uniqueness in order to be connected and sacrifice some connectedness in order to feel more unique. Imagine, for example, a volunteer named Julie. Part of her feeling of uniqueness revolves around her image of herself as a free-spirit. This manifests itself in a variety of ways, such as wearing unusual clothing and jewellery. Her organisation's values, however, are quite traditional, and it is an accepted group norm to dress conservatively. Julie is faced with a choice between dressing conservatively to gain a sense of connectedness, thus sacrificing some of her uniqueness, or to continue her unique style at the risk of becoming something of an outsider to the group. Neither of these courses of action is fully satisfactory to her.

Creating a positive climate is often difficult. It cannot be done without lots of interaction among group members. It cannot be done without shared values and a common purpose. It may require the services of an expert facilitator to lead a retreat in which people explore their differences and gain an understanding of each person's unique point of view. It is always enhanced by leaders talking up the strengths of individual members and their

> In a truly positive climate, people feel safe to be who they are. They can behave in an individual manner and yet feel supported by the group. People respect each other for their unique strengths and eccentricities. They support each other unconditionally.

contributions to the purpose of the group. It is maintained by leaders regarding as 'wrong' behaviour one person making fun of another or disparaging their accomplishments or desires.

It is also enhanced by encouraging the individual development of each volunteer. Provide people with maximum training. As they learn new skills, their sense of individual competence grows. A common way to do this is to send them to conferences and workshops to keep them up to date with the latest developments in their fields.

One good idea is to have volunteers research a topic and present their findings to the others. This enhances the presenter's feelings of uniqueness - their special knowledge is being imparted to others, while also creating connectedness. It creates an atmosphere that each team member can be depended on.

Effectiveness

Another aspect of positive self-esteem is a feeling that the volunteer is making a difference. This feeling is often throttled by traditional volunteer jobs. If people work in fragmented systems, doing menial tasks not connected to a final outcome, it is difficult for them to feel that they are making much of a difference. The self-esteem of people in such circumstances is reduced.

To feel effective, volunteers need to work on things that matter. If they are engaged in support activities, for example stuffing envelopes, they should be told the purpose of the mailing and the results that are achieved from it so they can feel they are having an effect on something worthwhile.

Part of feeling effective is feeling in control of one's life. Managers often take this away from people by trying to overly control their behaviour. Rather than defining results and allowing people some say in figuring out how to achieve them, managers tell people exactly what to do. When one human being attempts to control the behaviour of another, the result is rarely top performance.

As explained in previous chapters, you can produce feelings of effectiveness by making volunteers responsible for results. Volunteers then have the sense of being in charge of something meaningful. You can then allow people to control their own behaviour by giving them the authority to think.

The need to feel in control is often in conflict with a person's need for connectedness. People in teams sometimes yearn for more freedom of action. Their desire to influence others sometimes alienates other group members.

As Glasser points out in his book *Control Theory*, almost everyone

> To feel effective, volunteers need to work on things that matter. If they are engaged in support activities, for example stuffing envelopes, they should be told the purpose of the mailing and the results that are achieved from it so they can feel they are having an effect on something worthwhile.

goes through life trying to balance conflicting needs, making compromises that are never fully satisfactory. If you can create a situation in which these conflicting motivational needs are met simultaneously, you will unleash a tremendous sense of well-being in your volunteers and enthusiasm for the job.

Applying retention strategies to short term volunteers

For many reasons, short-term volunteering is not as rewarding as long-term — it doesn't provide the emotional satisfaction of really being an integral part of something. Short-term volunteering is to long-term as fast food is to a real meal: you can survive on it but you don't call it dining. Many short-termers may be engaging in sporadic volunteering as a sampling technique until they find the volunteer position which is right for them, practising 'comparison shopping'.

In the 1988 Gallup Poll on Giving and Volunteering in the United States, 14% of those volunteers who reported increasing their volunteer hours said they did so because of expanding interest and involvement in the work they were doing.

To take advantage of this, a smart volunteer coordinator should develop a series of entry-level, short-term jobs which provide the volunteer with the opportunity to see how they like working with the organisation, its staff, and its clientele. Once the volunteer is working in these 'starter' jobs, the volunteer coordinator should work on retention, slowly grooming the volunteer for more work and ensuring that the volunteer truly enjoys the work they are doing. Volunteers are curiously rational: they won't stay in jobs that aren't enjoyable, and they will stay in those that are.

Volunteers are curiously rational: they won't stay in jobs that aren't enjoyable, and they will stay in those that are.

Some evidence for the effects of this phenomenon is available from studies of volunteer behaviour. From this perspective, emphasis on volunteer retention is much more important than emphasis on recruitment. Rather than focusing on constantly bringing new volunteers into the system, with the concomitant expenditure of energy required for recruitment, screening, orientation and training, this approach would concentrate on maintenance of the existing volunteer force through retention of the incumbents. Over time, the organisation will benefit from the increased experience levels of its volunteers and from the lessened costs of recruiting newcomers.

There are three different ways of *'improving'* volunteer jobs to make them more interesting and involving.

❶ *Give them a great place to work*

The process for strengthening involvement necessarily varies from job to job and from volunteer to volunteer, but some factors are probably common to all situations. One of these is providing for the volunteer a rewarding job, where working facilities are satisfactory and social relationships are positive.

Some research has identified factors which might be important. A study of volunteer workers in three Israeli social service organisations found that organisational variables (such as adequate preparation for the task they were asked to do) and attitudinal variables (such as task achievement, relationships with other volunteers, and the nature of the work itself) were the best predictors of volunteer retention.

After analysing their data, *(see table on right)* Colony, Chen and Andrews noted:

'Perhaps the single most important finding reported in this study is the relatively high importance volunteers accord situational facilities...In addition to the intrinsic and extrinsic incentives associated with volunteer work, then, it appears that individuals strongly desire conditions and organisational settings that facilitate effective and efficient volunteer work.'

Roughly translated, this means that volunteers like good working conditions, just like the rest of us, and that volunteers tend to prefer jobs where the environment is friendly, supportive, and effective.

The factors which are key elements for each volunteer job will vary. A study of the Master Gardener volunteer programme identified three top perceived benefits which volunteers thought essential: receiving new sources of information, obtaining new gardening knowledge, and gaining access to experts and information. Note

COLONY, CHEN, & ANDREWS RANK & MEAN SCORES OF INDIVIDUAL ITEMS FOR ALL VOLUNTEERS

Rank		Mean
1	Helping others	3.83
2	Clearly defined responsibilities	3.58
3	Interesting work	3.53
4	Competence of supervisor	3.51
5	Supervisor guidance	3.47
6	Seeing results of my work	3.46
7	Working with a respected community organisation	3.43
8	Reasonable work schedule	3.41
9	Doing the things I do best	3.39
10	Suitable workload	3.22
11	Freedom to decide how to get work done	3.21
12	Chance to make friends	3.20
13	Pleasant physical surroundings	3.17
14	Opportunity to develop special skills/abilities	3.09
15	Challenging problems to solve	3.05
16	Convenient travel to and from volunteer work	2.94
17	Opportunity to work with professional staff	2.88
18	Volunteer recognition	2.49
19	Adequate reimbursement of out-of-pocket expenses	2.07
20	Chance to move to paid employment	1.50

This study identified the following factors as important to volunteers in any volunteer job. The factors are ranked from 1 to 4, with 1 being *'Not At All Important'* and 4 being *'Very Important.'*

Note that most of the top 10 items deal with the situation in which the volunteer work is performed and the design of the job itself: clear responsibilities, interesting work, effective supervision.

that none of these is 'altruistic'. Each factor involves a benefit which the volunteers felt to be of value to themselves and which was gained through volunteering and the additional training provided.

❷ *Give them what they don't have*

Another way of approaching the process of making a job more interesting is to look at it from the perspective of the potential volunteer. What is it, for example, that they want out of this volunteer job that they aren't getting from their current paid job?

A study of volunteers at three social service organisations tested the hypothesis that some people volunteer in order to satisfy needs that are not currently being met in their paid employment. The findings indicated that volunteers whose regular paid employment failed to satisfy their needs for psychological growth tended to be more satisfied with volunteering when it could satisfy those growth needs.

One of the conclusions was particularly intriguing: *'The study suggests that volunteers who perceive their paid jobs as relatively unfulfilling should be asked to do the more challenging work.'*

This would suggest that volunteer motivation could be improved by first analysing potential volunteer attitudes toward their current job to identify deficiencies, and then structuring volunteer assignments to fill the gaps. Variables that might be examined would include whether the paid job is worthwhile, interesting, satisfying, diverse, flexible, and allowed for such factors as social interaction, expression of leadership skills, etc. Sample questions which could be used during the volunteer interview would include:

♦   *'What do you get out of your current job?'*
♦   *'What do you not get to do sufficiently in your current job?'*
♦   *'What would your ideal job look like? '*
♦   *'What would you do in it, and what would you not do?'*

The prospective volunteer would be encouraged to identify elements of a possible volunteer job that would meet motivational needs not currently being met in their life and particularly not being met in their paid work. It would then become important to make sure that the volunteer job provided this perceived need.

❸ *Give them a good time*

Another way of thinking about more effective retention is to develop ways to let the volunteer have more 'fun'.

This is not quite as strange a notion as it might seem. Henderson has suggested that one way to view volunteering is as a 'leisure' activity – something which is done freely without expectation of monetary benefit. Volunteering and leisure have similar expected benefits: *'People want to do something interesting, to achieve something, meet people, have fun, learn new things, be refreshed, and relax.'* All of these factors might be examined as aspects of volunteer jobs which could be strengthened.

Focusing retention efforts on critical points

One way to encourage volunteer retention is to focus on critical points in the volunteer's cycle of relationships with the organisation. There are two critical periods:

The first six months

Studies of volunteer retention have determined that the first six months experience of a volunteer is critical towards their retention. The greatest loss of volunteers occurs during this period, as volunteers resign or simply drift away and disappear.

The loss probably occurs because new volunteers have approached the organisation with a set of expectations for what they will encounter and what they will be able to accomplish. During their initial contact with the organisation and its work, they will come face-to-face with the reality of the situation. If there is a significant gap between high mutual expectations and the actual situation encountered, the volunteer is more likely to reach a decision to depart.

Volunteer managers need to pay close attention to volunteers during this early period and help the transition through the normal ups and downs of this acclimatisation period. They should also ensure that the volunteer does not have problems created by being given an inappropriate job.

'Anniversaries'

Volunteers also require more attention at 'anniversaries,' such as annual evaluation dates, the end of large projects, or the completion of an agreed term of participation.

At these critical points, the volunteer is likely to engage in a re-

---

Henderson suggests that the volunteer manager focus on four areas to take advantage of the relationship between leisure and volunteering:

◆ The self-interest and recreational expectations of volunteers which might make volunteering more appealing to people.

◆ Providing volunteer opportunities which will be perceived as worthy leisure.

◆ Utilising the 'recreative aspects' of volunteering as a technique for recruitment.

◆ Matching a person's leisure expectations to potential outcomes associated with a volunteer experience.

The J.C. Penny survey alluded to earlier suggests that some aspects of leisure, such as enjoying activities conducted with one's social group, may be of particular significance in tapping this aspect of motivation.

evaluation of their service to the organisation, reconsidering their commitment to and interest in the work that they are doing. You can assist the volunteer in re-affirming that commitment by pro-actively assisting the volunteer in this analysis, helping the volunteer identify new interests and goals, and then suggesting possible jobs within the organisation that will help the volunteer obtain these new motivational objectives.

Do not assume that a volunteer who has been doing a job will always want to do that same job. Volunteers change over time, due both to changes in their own lives and to exposure to types of volunteer work. Periodically review what they are doing with them.

Don't forget the obvious

Two final comments about retention: the first is so obvious that many programmes not only ignore it, they do exactly the opposite. Since volunteers are coming to the organisation because they want to help, it is essential that you do everything you can to give volunteers work to do as soon as possible. Underutilisation creates serious retention problems, because motivated volunteers who are trying to be of assistance will feel useless if they are not actually involved in doing something. They will also lose any sense of relationship with the organisation over long periods of non-involvement. In the words of Hanawi: *'There is a minimal level of activity which is necessary for volunteers to feel connected to an organisation; there are individual variations in this critical level but certainly when a person's involvement falls below one or two hours a month, or when there is no continuity in the level of contact, volunteers will drift away.'*

The second is equally obvious: *when in doubt, ask the volunteer what they want to be doing.* Part of the original volunteer interview and part of every subsequent evaluation session should consist of ascertaining what the organisation might do that would meet the volunteer's motivations. This includes identifying the right job for the volunteer, but it also includes identifying what it would take for the volunteer to feel successful in the job. Questions such as: *'how can we show you we care?,' 'what would it take to make you feel successful in this job?,' 'who would you like to know about your accomplishments?',* are designed to uncover possible retention and recognition strategies. It is vitally necessary to keep exploring this area because the motivational needs of the volunteer will undoubtedly change over their lifetime and during the course of their relationship with the organisation.

RECOGNISING VOLUNTEERS

Volunteers must receive a sense of appreciation and reward for their contribution. This sense can be conveyed through a number of processes, including both formal and informal recognition systems.

> "when in doubt, ask the volunteer what they want to be doing"

Formal recognition systems

Formal recognition systems are comprised of the awards, certificates, plaques, pins, and recognition dinners or receptions to honour volunteer achievement. Many organisations hold an annual ceremony in which individual volunteers are singled out for their achievement.

In determining whether or not to establish such a formal ceremony, consider the following:

◆ *Is this being done to honour the volunteer, or so that staff can feel involved and can feel that they have shown their appreciation for volunteers?*

◆ *Is it real, and not stale or mechanical?*

◆ *Does it fit? Would the volunteers feel better if you spent the money on the needs of the clients rather than on an obligatory luncheon with dubious food?*

◆ *Can you make it a sense of celebration and a builder of team identity?*

Formal recognition systems are helpful mainly in satisfying the needs of the volunteer who has a need for community approval, but have little impact (and occasionally have a negative impact) on volunteers whose primary focus is helping the clientele. These volunteers may very well feel more motivated and honoured by a system which recognises the achievements of 'their' clients, and also recognises the contribution which the volunteer has made towards this achievement.

Informal recognition practices

The most effective volunteer recognition occurs in the day-to-day interchange between the volunteer and the organisation through the staff giving their sincere appreciation and thanks for the work being done by the volunteer.

This type of recognition is more powerful in part because it is much more frequent – a once-a-year dinner does not carry the same impact as 365 days of good working relationships.

The intention of day-to-day recognition is to convey a constant sense of appreciation and belonging to the volunteer. This sense can be better conveyed by

---

Day-to-day recognition may include such items as:

◆ Saying 'thank you'

◆ Involving the volunteer in decisions that affect them

◆ Asking about the volunteer's family and showing an interest in their 'outside' life

◆ Making sure that volunteers receive equal treatment to that given staff

◆ Sending a note of appreciation to the volunteer's family

◆ Allowing the volunteer to increase their skills by attending training

◆ Recommending the volunteer for promotion to a more responsible job

◆ Celebrating the volunteer's anniversary with the organisation

the thousands of small interactions that compose daily life than it can be conveyed in an annual event.

Recognition can begin quite early. A card of welcome sent to a new volunteer, or a small welcome party conveys an immediate sense of appreciation.

Matching recognition to types of volunteers

It is also possible to think about systems of volunteer recognition that are appropriate to particular types of volunteers:

❶ *By motivational orientation*

One could think about recognition which was more appropriate for different basic motivational needs, as follows:

Achievement-oriented volunteers

- ◆ Ideal result of recognition is additional training or more challenging tasks.
- ◆ Subject for recognition is best linked to a very specific accomplishment
- ◆ Phrasing of recognition through 'Best,' 'Most' awards
- ◆ Recognition decision should include 'Checkpoints' or 'Records'
- ◆ Awardee should be selected by co-workers

Affiliation-oriented volunteers

- ◆ Recognition should be given at group event
- ◆ Recognition should be given in presence of peers, family, other bonded groupings
- ◆ Recognition item or award should have a 'Personal Touch'
- ◆ Recognition should be organisational in nature, given by the organisation
- ◆ Recognition should be voted by peers
- ◆ If primary affiliative bonding is with client, not others in the organisation, then the client should take part in the recognition, through a personal note of thanks or as presenter of the award

Power-oriented volunteers

- ◆ Key aspect of recognition is 'Promotion, conveying greater access to authority or information
- ◆ Recognition should be commendation from 'Names'

◆ Recognition should be announced to community at large, put in newspaper

◆ Recognition decision should be made by the organisation's leadership

❷ *By style of volunteering*

Recognition might also vary as between long-term and short-term volunteers:

Long-term volunteer

◆ Recognition with and by the group

◆ Recognition items make use of group symbols

◆ Recognition entails greater power, involvement, information about the organisation

◆ Presenter of recognition is a person in authority

Short-term volunteer

◆ Recognition is given in immediate work unit or social group

◆ Recognition is 'portable;' something which the volunteer can take with them when they leave – a present, photograph or other memorabilia of experience, training, etc.

◆ Recognition is provided via home or work – letter to employer, church or family

◆ Presenter is either the immediate supervisor or the client

You should note that an 'ideal' recognition system might require a mixture of different procedures in order to have something for every type of volunteer. This is not unusual and is quite appropriate. Many organisations fail to do this, with interesting results. Consider, for example, an all-too-typical organisation that gives its volunteer awards according to the amount of time donated, a 'longevity' prize. If you're a short-term volunteer how do you feel about this system? Or if your busy schedule limits the time you can offer? Could you possibly ever 'win' under these rules? What would this type of award suggest to you about the value that the organisation places upon your own contribution?

IDEAS FOR RECOGNITION

Here are some examples of different levels of recognition activity:

Daily means of providing recognition:

◆ Saying 'Thank you.'

◆ Telling them they did a good job.

◆ Suggesting they join you for coffee.

◆ Asking for their opinions.

◆ Greeting them when they come in the morning.

◆ Showing interest in their personal interests.

◆ Smiling when you see them.

◆ Bragging about them to your boss (in their presence).

◆ Jotting small thank you notes to them.

◆ Having a refreshment with them after work.

◆ Saying something positive about their personal qualities.

Intermediate means of providing recognition:

◆ Taking them to lunch.

◆ Providing food at volunteer meetings.

◆ Letting them put their names on the products they produce.

◆ Buying the first round of beer for 'the best crew of the month.'

◆ Writing them a letter of commendation (with copies to personnel file and other appropriate people.)

◆ Getting a local radio station to mention them.

◆ Putting them on important task forces or committees.

◆ Giving the best parking space to the 'employee of the month.'

◆ Posting graphic displays, showing progress toward targets.

◆ Mentioning major contributors by name in your status reports to senior management.

◆ Asking them to present their results to those ' higher up ' .

- Giving permission to go to a seminar, convention, or professional meeting, if possible at the organisation's expense.

- Writing articles about their performance for newsletters or newspapers.

- Asking them to present a training session to co-workers.

- Decorating their work area on their birthday.

- Asking your boss to write them a letter of thanks.

- Celebrating major accomplishments.

- Inviting them to represent you at important meetings.

- Putting their picture on the bulletin board with news of their accomplishments.

- Cutting out articles and cartoons they might be interested in.

- Organising informal chats with organisation leadership.

Major means of providing recognition:

- Making special caps, shirts, belt buckles or lapel badges honouring the group.

- Encouraging them to write an article about some accomplishment at work.

- Giving a plaque, certificate, or trophy for being best employee, best crew, most improved results, etc.

- Offering tuition assistance.

- Buying them good equipment.

- Getting their picture in the paper for outstanding accomplishment.

- Giving additional responsibilities and a new title.

- Renting newspaper space to thank them.

- Putting up a banner celebrating a major accomplishment.

- Honouring them for years of service to the organisation.

- Giving them a bigger office.

- Enlisting them in training staff and other volunteers.

- Involving them in the annual planning process.

RULES FOR RECOGNITION

Whatever mix of recognition system you utilise, remember the following rules:

❶ Give it or else.

The need for recognition is very important to most people. If volunteers don't get recognition for productive participation, only bad things can happen. The least of these is that they will feel unappreciated and drop out. Alternatively, they may start getting recognition from their peers (in the form of attention, laughter, camaraderie) for snide remarks and other more serious disruptive behaviour.

❷ Give it frequently.

The most common complaint of volunteers is that they don't get enough recognition from staff. Staff are usually surprised by this and can often site examples in which they have given recognition to volunteers. The reason for this discrepancy of perception is that recognition has a short shelf life. Its effects start to wear off after a few days, and after several weeks of not hearing anything positive, volunteers start to wonder if they are appreciated. Giving recognition once a year to a volunteer at a recognition banquet is certainly not enough.

❸ It must be varied.

One of the implications of the previous rule is that you need a variety of methods of showing appreciation to volunteers. Fortunately, there are hundreds of methods. Recognition can be categorised into four major types:

◆ From a person for the work the volunteer did

Examples include saying 'You did a great job on this' or writing them a letter to that effect.

◆ From a person for being part of the organisation.

Examples include birthday celebrations or personal compliments such as 'I am impressed by your uniformly pleasant attitude.' These have nothing to do with the volunteer's work performance but are expressions of appreciation of them as a person.

◆ From the organisation for work the volunteer did.

Examples would include a plaque commemorating their work on a project or being honoured as 'Volunteer of the Month' because of their outstanding achievements.

◆ From the organisation for being part of the team.

Examples include a plaque commemorating years of service or being featured in a newsletter article that tells interesting personal facts about the volunteer but is not written due to particular job performance.

All of these types are valid. Some appeal more to some people than to others.

④ It must be honest.

Don't give praise unless you mean it. If you praise substandard performance, the praise you give to others for good work will not be valued. If a volunteer is performing poorly, you might be able to give them honest recognition for their effort or for some personality trait.

⑤ It should be given to the person, not to the work.

This is a subtle but important distinction. If volunteers organise a fund-raising event, for example, and you praise the event, the volunteers may feel some resentment. Make sure you connect the volunteer's name to it. It is better to say 'John, Betty, and Megan did a great job organising this event,' than to say 'This event was really well-organised.'

⑥ It should be appropriate to the achievement.

Small accomplishments should be praised with low-effort methods, large accomplishments should get something more. For example, if a volunteer tutor teaches a child to spell 'Cat' today, we could say 'well done!' If s/he writes a grant that doubles our funding, a banner lauding the accomplishment might be more appropriate.

⑦ It should be consistent.

If two volunteers are responsible for similar achievements, they ought to get similar recognition. If one gets his or her picture in the lobby and another gets an approving nod, the latter may feel resentment. This does not mean that the recognition has to be exactly the same, but that it should be the result of similar effort on your part. Otherwise certain volunteers will come to be regarded as 'favourites,' a stigma they may grow to dread.

⑧ It must be timely.

Praise for work should come as soon as possible after the achievement. Don't save up your recognition for the annual banquet. If volunteers have to wait months before hearing any word of praise, they may develop resentment for lack of praise in the meantime.

⑨ It should be individualised as much as possible.

Different people like different things. One might respond favourably to football tickets, another might find them useless. In order to provide effective recognition, you need to get to know your people and what they will respond to positively.

⑩ Pay attention to what you want more of.

Too often your staff pay most attention to volunteers who are having difficulty. Unfortunately, this may result in ignoring good performers. We are not suggesting that you ignore sub-par volunteers, just that you make sure that you praise the efforts of those who are doing a good job.

IF ALL ELSE FAILS, DO THINGS CORRECTLY

The final answer to volunteer retention and recognition is quite simple – operate a well-managed programme. Volunteers, like the rest of us, tend to make rational decisions about the allocation of their time; they will strive to spend it in settings where they obtain value. This value may be the social aspects, the work objectives, the situational settings, or a combination of all of these. Programmes that can give volunteers a work setting in which they can do good work, in a good setting, with good people uniquely positioned to provide this sense of value and accomplishment, and often can do so in ways that paid work settings are not able to provide. The principles of good volunteer management described in other chapters outline the actions which can enable a volunteer programme to provide this positive environment. Always remember McCurley's Law of Volunteer Retention:

'The longer a volunteer is around the more likely they are to notice when the elements of good volunteer management are not in place. The honeymoon is over.'

> **The longer a volunteer is around the more likely they are to notice when the elements of good volunteer management are not in place. The honeymoon is over.**

Good volunteer-staff relations are critical – for all organisations – and of particular concern when you are introducing volunteering into the organisation or to a specific project.

THINKING ABOUT VOLUNTEERS FROM THE STAFF'S PERSPECTIVE

Imagine for a moment that you are a staff person who has never before worked with a computer. At a staff meeting the director of your organisation announces that s/he believes that computerisation is the only answer to the enormous workload that your organisation faces, and intends to obtain as much computer equipment as possible for staff, none of whom at this point is computer literate. S/he announces that s/he has just hired a Director of Computer Operations to 'get the organisation moving on this.'

Shortly after this meeting, the new Director of Computer Operations walks into your office, deposits a computer on your desk, says *'Here's your new computer, hope you enjoy it!'* , and walks out. There is no instructional manual, no training session, you have no knowledge about how to operate the machine, and little space in your office to accommodate it.

◆ *What would you do in this situation...?*

◆ *Bang at the keys until something happened?*

◆ *Place the computer in the corner and use it as a plant stand?*

◆ *How would you feel if you were the staff person, given a possible resource that you don't fully understand and may even resent for the changes it imposes on your work style?*

It may sound strange to say, but volunteers and computers have a lot in common: each resource has suffered from haphazard attempts to implement its use within voluntary organisations.

> Topics covered include:
>
> ◆ **The role of the volunteer manager**
>
> ◆ **Dealing with staff concerns**
>
> ◆ **An eight-part system for good volunteer-staff relations**
>
> ◆ **An important role for senior management**
>
> ◆ **The need to create an organisational climate that recognises and respects volunteer usage.**

Each resource is complicated and multi-faceted. Each requires specific skills on the part of the staff who will be using it. And each, to be most effective, needs to be customised for the particular usages, setting, and personalities involved.

About the only differences between a computer and a volunteer from a strict management standpoint are that volunteers are more complex (they can do a greater variety of things, if operated properly) and they are less forgiving. A volunteer, for example, doesn't take well to being asked to stand in the corner and serve as a plant stand until needed.

This is a round-about way of explaining that staff difficulties in working with volunteers – whether they include active opposition, passive resistance, or simple inability to achieve creative usage - are probably not really the fault of any of the staff.

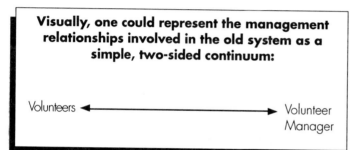

Visually, one could represent the management relationships involved in the old system as a simple, two-sided continuum:

Volunteers ◄————————► Volunteer Manager

For the most part, many staff who are being encouraged to make use of volunteers are in an equivalent position to a person being given a computer and told: *'Bang the keys until something happens.'*

No matter how well meaning the member of staff is, they are unlikely to accomplish much. They are likely to become frustrated. And they are very likely to damage the equipment.

THE CHANGE IN VOLUNTEER UTILISATION PATTERNS

To understand why this lack of ability to work with volunteers is so damaging, you must realise the immense changes that have taken place in volunteer involvement patterns during the past decade. *(see diagram above and overleaf)*.

Twenty years ago most volunteer departments in the United States operated, for the most part, on their own. Usually a volunteer coordinator (either paid or unpaid) supervised the activities of volunteers engaged in a variety of projects or activities.

Usually these volunteers were engaged in programme activities that were somewhat 'separate' from the other organisational operations. The volunteer coordinator was responsible for almost all recruitment, job development, supervision of 'the' volunteers.

The volunteer coordinator was essentially responsible for everything that related to the volunteers. In some cases this could result in rather strange management systems where one volunteer coordinator was supposed to be 'in charge of' hundreds or even thousands of volunteers.

As volunteer involvement has become more sophisticated, this situation has changed considerably. Volunteers have 'diffused' throughout the structure of the organisation, become a more integral part of it, and sometimes assumed tasks and responsibilities that had previously been done by paid staff. As new activities were undertaken by the volunteers, they began to work more in partnership with staff, operating as 'aides' or members of teams, or simply as assigned workers to a staff department. They began to work regularly 'with' and 'for' other members of staff than the volunteer coordinator. In some cases they have been totally seconded to other staff.

This new system of volunteers working more directly with individual staff has totally changed the dynamics of effective volunteer management within the organisation.

This three-sided relationship is much more complex than the two-sided continuum. There are two major differences which this new system creates:

◆ A requirement that the volunteer manager view his or her job in a quite different fashion. As you can see from the connective lines of the triangle, the volunteer director 'links' both to volunteers and to staff. This means that work must be done with both to be successful.

◆ A realisation that the line relationship between the staff and the volunteers is the primary line of management and supervision. If volunteers work on a day-to-day basis with staff, whether through an assignment with a single staff person, or in conjunction with several staff, then it is the quality of that management and interpersonal interaction which will determine whether the volunteer is effectively and satisfactorily involved.

The operational relationships will vary in different organisations. Generally, the larger the organisation the more likely that volunteers will be working more directly with staff. It is quite apparent, however, that this is the most effective method of achieving optimal volunteer usage.

Think back to the computer illustration. If a staff person is provided with a computer, does the Director of Computer Operations attempt to operate the keyboard for each staff person?

> A volunteer, for example, doesn't take well to being asked to stand in the corner and serve as a plant stand until needed...

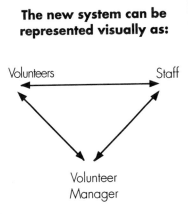

The new system can be represented visually as:

Volunteers   Staff

Volunteer Manager

Obviously not; and, the idea is ridiculous. Why, then, should we not also expect the staff to 'operate' the volunteers with whom they work?

For volunteer use to be effective, each staff member must understand and be able to implement volunteer management. They must have the capacity to comprehend the diversity of the volunteer workforce, to create imaginative and meaningful jobs for volunteers, and to effectively lead and supervise those volunteers with whom they work.

They must become, in essence, *'Managers of Volunteers.'*

NEW ROLES FOR THE VOLUNTEER DIRECTOR

And, in turn, volunteer directors must realise that preparing staff for these new responsibilities may necessitate a change in their own role. One way of explaining this shift is simply to note the subtle but significant difference between two phrases:

Director of Volunteers

Director of Volunteer Services

The first, *'Director of Volunteers,'* implies a person who 'directs' volunteers. It is the person responsible for everyday management and supervision of volunteers. In our computer analogy, the equivalent phrase would be *'Computer Operator.'*

The second, *'Director of Volunteer Services,'* indicates the person who is responsible for overall operations involving volunteers, but who does not manage each individual volunteer. Instead they enable, assist, and prepare each member of staff to make effective use of their own volunteers. In the computer analogy this would be the *'Director of Computer Operations.'*

What is needed is for volunteer managers to take a broader interpretation of their roles, viewing themselves as being responsible for the system of volunteer involvement within the organisation, which includes working closely with both volunteers and staff.

Alas, in the real world, this process is made somewhat more difficult. Quite frequently volunteer managers lack the real or apparent authority to *'direct'* anyone, much less senior organisation staff.

This lack of power makes it necessary for the successful volunteer manager to approach the role somewhat differently, assuming the guise of a *'consultant'*, one who helps when needed and who does not, and usually cannot, order anyone to do anything.

The consultant, in a situation of this sort, engages in two types of teaching behaviour:

- The first is **diagnosis.** In this context that means working with staff, sometimes on an individual basis, to help identify the ways in which volunteers can assist them in accomplishing the work within their purview. The key element in this process lies in showing staff how to think about volunteers in such a way that they can continue to think of appropriate and creative usages for volunteers.

- The second is **instruction.** This would involve educating staff about the requirements and techniques of working effectively with volunteers. In essence, the volunteer manager turns the staff into 'volunteer operators,' knowledgeable about both the overall system of volunteer involvement in the organisation and supervision of individual volunteers.

The volunteer manager will then identify, recommend and implement all the organisational actions which are needed to make it possible for staff to accomplish the tasks and activities identified during the diagnosis and instructional phase.

In all of this, the volunteer manager, acting as a consultant, concentrates on working with staff, not in attempting to coerce them. The point is to persuade and empower staff to think about volunteers from the perspective of a trained 'volunteer manager'.

And, inevitably, much as knowledge of, and even affection for, computers has blossomed among staff, so you can succeed in introducing the same improvement in their relationships with the volunteers they are working with.

DEALING WITH STAFF CONCERNS

A good volunteer manager will begin by recognising that staff may have legitimate fears or concerns about the deployment of volunteers.

> ### Staff concerns may be:
> - A fear of loss of control
> - A fear of diminished quality of service
> - A fear that volunteers will be unreliable
> - A fear of increased legal problems
>
> ### The concerns may be personal in nature:
> - A resentment of increased work load
> - A fear of loss of a job
> - A fear of having to manage volunteers without experience to do so

The role of the volunteer manager is to determine the concerns of the staff and then turn these concerns into a sense of confidence among the staff that the volunteers will be a useful addition to the organisation.

In general, this means imparting two feelings to staff:

❶ A sense of benefits greater than the difficulties or problems

❷ A feeling of control over the situation

Staff are more likely to be 'satisfied' with the volunteers they will be working with if they can perceive that the return to them is greater than the effort involved, and if they believe that they will be closely involved in making decisions that affect how they are to work with the volunteers.

In dealing with staff concerns, it is wise to note that your natural instincts (to 'fight and win') may be disastrous. Many volunteer managers attempt to deal with staff concerns through throwing their weight around, often through seeking a top management mandate that 'volunteers *will* be assigned to all staff.'

This approach is fatal. It will leave the staff seeking revenge for what has been imposed upon them, and they will exercise this revenge upon the only available target – the volunteers.

Such a situation can also involve you in unpleasant political games. These affect the morale of the organisation in adverse ways. In cases where there is a lot of conflict among staff, where there is a 'war zone' atmosphere, volunteer turnover will be higher. If a volunteer senses tension and conflict in the organisation, they will be deterred from continuing to work. Volunteer time is discretionary time, and most people prefer to spend their discretionary time in a pleasant environment.

Another fatal approach is the use of criticism. Arguing with staff is futile; telling them five reasons why they are wrong is futile. Many of the concerns of staff will not be built entirely upon logic, and, indeed, may not even be directly related to the volunteer programme. Directly confronting staff may only produce a defensiveness that will turn to hostility if you continue to push the issue.

CREATING A SYSTEM OF GOOD VOLUNTEER-STAFF RELATIONS

A system for good volunteer-staff relations requires the following eight elements to be in place:

❶ Overall policy on volunteer utilisation

The organisation should have an overall policy on volunteer use, expressing why the organisation employs volunteers.

> ❝ **Volunteer time is discretionary time, and most people prefer to spend their discretionary time in a pleasant environment** ❞

Reasons may include:

◆ Provide community outreach and input
◆ Gain additional human resources
◆ Cost savings
◆ Supplement expertise of staff
◆ Allow involvement of client groups
◆ Demonstrate community support
◆ Act as conduit to funders
◆ Provide personal touch in services to clients

The policy should provide a clear rationale, which can be used in explaining the volunteer programme both to staff and to potential volunteers. It indicates to the staff that the volunteer programme is not just an emergency measure dreamed up one weekend by a desperate Executive Director, but is one which fits within the overall mission of the organisation. The policy should:

◆ Be adopted and supported by trustees and other top policy makers
◆ Be integrated into overall organisation plans and budgets
◆ Encourage, but not mandate, staff involvement.

That last point is often overlooked, but is crucial. It is impossible to force staff to work effectively with volunteers. There are too many ways for staff to sabotage volunteer effort to think that staff can ever be coerced into productively using volunteers when they do not want to. Even indifference of staff will quickly communicate itself to volunteers, who will equally quickly decide not to be where they are not wanted. Mandatory policies create resistance, and you will only be asking for trouble if you attempt to force compliance. Plan to work through rewards for productive staff, not punishments. (A sample of such a policy on volunteers can be found in Chapter Two, *'Planning a Volunteer Programme'*).

You might also want to make sure that staff understand the need for volunteers, and understand that the volunteers are being involved to help, not hurt, staff.

CASE STUDY

from brochure entitled 'Make Your Mark–Volunteer', which the Oregon Department of Human Resources distributes to its staff:

What's in it for me?

You can use the supervision of volunteers as experience when you are applying for promotions. By using tools such as position descriptions, training, evaluation and feedback, you develop your own management skills. Involving volunteers in your problem solving and planning may help you gain a unique and valuable source of contributions and ideas. With the everyday workloads, it's hard to get to special projects and activities. Volunteers may be able to help you accomplish some of the things that you have had to put aside. At the same time you help yourself, you are helping volunteers reach their own goals.

Can volunteers replace paid staff?

It isn't fair to volunteers or paid staff of your organisation to use volunteers to replace paid personnel. Volunteer staff can supplement and complement the work that is being done by employees. Also, volunteers can help you catch up on things that are backlogged and/or help extend some of the services that you provide.

Can I depend on volunteers to be professional?

Most volunteers have a professional attitude about their work. They take their responsibilities seriously, and uphold the policies of the organisation and other requirements such as confidentiality. Identifying the assignment and carefully matching the volunteer to the job will help to eliminate future problems. Good direction from you and other staff with periodic monitoring and feedback will help the volunteer serve professionally.

Such a communication*(see case study on page 141)* can pro-actively address staff concerns and smooth the way for a successful staff-volunteer interaction.

❷ Assessment of staff capabilities

The more you know about your staff, the better you can design a system which takes into account their individual characteristics. A very effective preliminary tool is a quick survey of staff attitudes and experience with volunteers. This should seek to ascertain the following:

◆ *Previous staff experience with volunteering.*

This includes their own experience as volunteers, their previous work in an organisation which used volunteers, and any previous experience in supervising volunteers.

◆ *Staff attitudes towards the use of volunteers.*

This would include the opinions of staff about the perceived need for volunteers, and any fears or recommendations about what jobs would be appropriate or inappropriate for volunteers. It would also include staff perceptions of what needs to happen before volunteers are brought into the organisation. (A sample survey is provided in Appendix B)

❸ Staff orientation to the volunteer programme

Staff need to learn the 'system' for volunteer involvement within the organisation. This would include educating them about the following:

◆ Rationale for using volunteers
◆ Brief history of volunteer programme
◆ Explanation of types of volunteers and the jobs they do
◆ Description of the contributions of volunteers
◆ In-depth explanation of role of the staff in all aspects of working with volunteers

This 'orientation' might actually be provided in different ways and at different times. Part might be given to each new staff member. Part might be given as staff begin to be involved with volunteers. It may be given either in a formal or informal setting, either in a workshop or one-on-one. It is very effective to include successful managers of volunteers and volunteers as co-presenters during these sessions.

Some information may be provided in writing, as the example over the page from the Oregon Department of Human Service brochure illustrates.

CASE STUDY

FROM THE OREGON DEPT OF HUMAN SERVICE

Can the volunteer programme help clients I can't help?

Helping people is what our organisations are all about. The Volunteer Programme can be a place to turn when you are unable to help a client. Sometimes volunteers will be able to meet some of the client's needs or assist you in identifying resources in the community. The Volunteer Programme can make the tough part of your job just a little easier.

What happens when you make a referral?

When you make a volunteer request, the local Volunteer Programme Supervisor's (VPS) response will depend on the type of request. If the help you need is available immediately, the request will be filled quickly. If the service, volunteer or resource isn't available, the Volunteer Programme will try to recruit, interview and register volunteers for you, or they may help you locate and access other resources. If the request is inappropriate for volunteer involvement, the VPS will call you to discuss available alternatives. Since the Volunteer Programme serves four different divisions (Adult and Family Services Division, Children's Services Division, Mental Health Division, and Senior Services Division) every effort will be made to provide equal access to the services available. Priorities for your Volunteer Programme are established by a local Volunteer Programme board, with representatives from each organisation.

How hard can it be to find lots of volunteers?

Our Volunteer Programme is competing with dozens of organisations in the recruitment of volunteers. Also, we're choosy; we want only the best. We screen all volunteer applicants to make sure they are appropriate and capable of serving our clients. Your help is important in keeping and attracting volunteers. Meaningful opportunities and positive experiences will keep present volunteers involved in our programme. Also those same opportunities and experiences will help us find new volunteers. Nothing attracts like success. We welcome your help. If you would like to register as a volunteer or know of someone else who would be interested, talk to your nearest Volunteer Programme. Our recruitment process is ongoing.

What does it take to get a volunteer going on a project?

Volunteers come to us with a vast range of abilities, experiences, and interests. Some may be well equipped for the jobs and others may require some training. Every volunteer you work with will need clear instructions in order to do the best job for you. The effort you spend training a volunteer and outlining clear performance expectations will make the experience positive and productive for both of you.

Also, since most volunteers have lots of other commitments, working out a mutually agreeable schedule is very important for both of you. Good planning helps ensure success for everyone, and encourages the volunteer to consider future projects that you may have.

❹ Personalised volunteer job creation

Ultimately, volunteer retention lies in having jobs which are interesting and rewarding enough that volunteers really enjoy doing them. No recruitment campaign can compensate for boring volunteer jobs. This means that there needs to be a process in place for creating jobs which are meaningful to the member of staff who will be working with the volunteer (i.e., they really help out) and meaningful to potential volunteers. This process will work in three ways:

Providing staff with ideas for volunteer use

You might explain the options for using volunteers, for example, produce a guide for staff which sparks their thinking about volunteer jobs by explaining various possibilities.

You could explain the different ways in which volunteers might help:

◆ Are there areas of work that staff don't want to do? This may be because staff are not skilled in that type of work, or are too skilled for the work, or else simply have a preference to concentrate their efforts in something else.

◆ Are there areas in which there is too much work for staff to do alone, and for which you might create volunteer assistants to supplement staff resources? These assistants might work directly with one member of staff or could do tasks that benefit all staff.

◆ Are there areas in which you can extend services because volunteers would enable the organisation to begin work that you cannot now even consider undertaking?

You might also suggest the creation of volunteer jobs based on the recipients of the service. Consider the following:

◆ Jobs that are of direct assistance to an individual client (counselling, visiting, buddying, mentoring, etc.)

◆ Office administrative help (information services, filing, messengers, etc.)

◆ Direct assistance to staff (research, training, computer help, etc.)

◆ Outreach (speakers panel, fundraising, marketing and evaluation, research, etc.)

You might also want to suggest some considerations that staff should bear in mind as they think about potential jobs:

◆ The work must be meaningful and significant, both to the organisation and to the clientele. The work must be needed and should be interesting to the person doing it. This means that each volunteer job must have a 'Goal' or a 'Purpose' that the volunteer can accomplish and can feel good about having achieved.

◆ The volunteer ought to be able to feel some 'ownership' and 'responsibility' for the job. Volunteers are not robots, but must feel that they have some input into and control over the work they are asked to do. This will mean including the volunteer in the flow of information and decision-making within the office.

◆ The work must fit a part-time situation (for a part-time volunteer). Either the work must be small enough in scope to be productively undertaken in a few hours a week, or else it must be designed to be shared among a group of volunteers.

> *The more flexible the timeframe of the volunteer job, the greater the likelihood that there will be someone willing to undertake it. Think about the following as different options for the job:*
>
> ◆ **Can the work be done to a totally flexible schedule at the discretion of the volunteer?**
>
> ◆ **Are there set hours during the week when the volunteer is needed?**
>
> ◆ **Could the work be done in the evenings or at weekends?**
>
> ◆ **Must the work be done on-site or at the office?**

◆ Volunteers must be 'worked with'. They should be assigned to work with staff who are capable of supervising their activities in a productive fashion, and of providing on-going direction, evaluation and feedback. What arrangements will you need to make in order to ensure satisfactory supervision?

And you may want to provide some helpful hints to staff, hints that would be helpful both to them and to you.

Assisting staff in creating volunteer jobs

The best method to assist staff in developing volunteer jobs is for the volunteer manager to interview each member of staff. The purpose of this interview is to match what the staff know about their work situation with what the volunteer manager knows about volunteers.

The following questions will generate ideas about possible tasks that volunteers might perform:

◆ What are the types of things you are in charge of? What kinds of things do you do to accomplish this work?

◆ What parts of your job do you really like to do?

◆ What parts of your job do you not like to do?

◆ What kind of knowledge or training would a person need to do this job?

◆ What would you do if you had a full-time staff person assigned as your assistant?

◆ What are some things that you would like to get done that you never have time to get around to?

◆ Is there anything that you've always wanted to learn how to do?

◆ Is it possible volunteers might be able to do some of the things you could do by working under your supervision?

It is also important to ask questions that will help with other parts of the volunteer involvement process:

◆ How might you ensure that the volunteers have the necessary training or knowledge?

◆ Are there any changes in the way you work that you think you will need to make in order to use volunteers?

◆ What changes in office operations should be made for volunteers to work here?

◆ What resources will you need in order for you to work with volunteers?

◆ What types of people do you prefer to work with?

◆ What types of people do you prefer not to work with?

While time-consuming, this interviewing process is by far the most productive method for developing ideas for meaningful and significant volunteer jobs, as well as providing the volunteer manager with vital information about matching and preparing volunteers. Chapter Three contains more information on how to assist staff in developing volunteer jobs.

HELPING STAFF CONTINUE TO DEVELOP INNOVATIVE JOBS

The job development process is never-ending. New ideas should be continuously provided to staff. Among the ways to do this are:

❶ Talent advertising:
disseminating information about volunteers who have recently joined the organisation with particular skills or expertise.

❷ Success stories:
highlighting examples of innovative usage of volunteers, often best done by showing the 'success' that staff have had in achieving some new goal or solving some problem through the involvement of volunteers

❸ Job upgrading:
organising scheduled evaluation sessions of volunteers to re-examine assignments and re-shape the job to take into account the growth and development of the volunteer.

❺ Early monitoring of volunteer placements

Staff who are afraid of a loss of quality control will be made more comfortable if they are included in the selection and induction process. Allow staff to help develop the criteria by which volunteers will be chosen, to participate in interviewing potential volunteers for their department, and to design and present portions of the volunteer training sessions.

Initial assignments for the volunteer can be on a trial basis. It would be irrational to assume following a 30-minute interview that you know precisely where this particular volunteer will be most effective. It is far better to give a temporary assignment, with a review scheduled for 30 days later. During this period, the volunteer can conduct a 'test drive' of the job and of the organisation, and determine if it matches his or her needs. The staff member who works with the volunteer can see if the volunteer has the qualifications and commitment required for the job. The volunteer manager can see that the volunteer and the member of staff have those essential elements of 'fit' that are essential to a mutually productive working relationship. The experience of this initial 'trial period' can then be used to finalise the placement of the volunteer. If changes need to be made, then it is much better to do them at this early stage than to wait until disaster strikes.

You will also need to monitor the member of staff providing 'on-the-job' training for the volunteer.

6 Staff control & responsibility in volunteer management

Once staff become accustomed to the idea of supervising 'their' volunteers, the majority will quickly become quite happy to accept this responsibility. The role of the volunteer manager is to teach them how to do this correctly, particularly as managing volunteers is different from managing paid staff, and to assist them in dealing with problem situations.

Be sure that you clarify the web of relationships between the volunteer, the member of staff and the volunteer manager. The member of staff must understand whether supervision is being done by themselves or by the volunteer manager. They must understand who is in charge of what, who is responsible for what, and what should happen if things go wrong. Who, for example, is in charge of firing an unsatisfactory volunteer? The member of staff? The volunteer manager? Is it a unilateral decision or a joint one? Is there any appeal or grievance procedure?

The extent of staff involvement will vary, depending upon the particular member of staff's own comfort and desire for management responsibilities. Even if the volunteer manager still 'controls' and supervises the volunteer, an effort should be made to make the members of staff feel a part of the supervisory team and to keep them informed about what is happening. You can do this by 'asking their advice' from time to time about how the volunteer should be treated, or inquiring as to how they think the volunteer is doing at the job. The organisation might also create set standards for staff supervision of volunteers (see case study over page).

CASE STUDY

FROM CATHOLIC CHARITIES
OF THE ARCHDIOCESE OF ST PAUL AND MINNEAPOLIS:

Minimum standards for supervisors of volunteers

We ask the volunteer supervisor to:

1 Attend required volunteer supervisor orientation/training.

2 Work with volunteer coordinator to clearly define volunteer positions which the supervisor is requesting (including duties, qualifications, and time commitment to fulfil the position). Keep volunteer coordinator informed of changes in job description.

3 Participate with the volunteer coordinator in the selection of volunteers for the specific position.

4 Provide specific on-site orientation and training for volunteers.

5 Assure regular contact with volunteers for whom you are responsible, and provide a minimum of annual formal evaluation session.

6 Communicate key information to volunteers which will affect the volunteer's performance (i.e. current operating information, changes in schedules, training, meeting dates, and changes in client status).

7 Assure report of volunteer's hours/impact to the volunteer coordinator.

8 Participate in formal and informal volunteer recognition activities.

9 Notify the volunteer coordinator of any problems or questions regarding a volunteer as soon as they become evident and prior to any decision to terminate.

10 Advise the volunteer coordinator when a volunteer terminates and/or has a change in volunteer status.

Supervisors of volunteers exceed expectations by:

1 Attending additional training regarding supervision.

2 Assisting the volunteer coordinator in recruitment of volunteers and being aware of organisational volunteer needs.

3 Designing and implementing the volunteer training and training materials.

4 Contributing to the volunteer's professional growth, including such things as resume writing, career laddering, reference letters, and special trainings.

5 Planning and implementing formal and informal recognition activities for volunteers.

6 Along with the volunteer coordinator, solving problems around potential issues/problems regarding volunteers and the volunteer programme.

7 Engaging with the volunteer coordinator in the annual planning process for the volunteer programme.

8 Participating in the divisional volunteer programme by serving on a task force or advisory committee.

❼ Feedback & recognition

The final element in a system for staff involvement is continuing to demand more volunteer help. This includes:

◆ Providing managerial information to staff on quantities and patterns of volunteer use.

◆ Showing examples of successful and innovative use of volunteers

◆ Implementing rewards and recognition for successful staff managers of volunteers.

Rewards for staff may range from formal recognition by the organisation of their accomplishment to increased chances for promotion, and some recognition of their skills (by their inclusion in volunteer management activities, training, staff orientations, etc).

❽ On-going relationship building

What you are trying to create is an overall organisational climate that recognises and respects volunteer usage. This means that true recognition should occur throughout the management process. Including volunteer use in overall evaluations of the organisation's accomplishments, or evaluating staff in their proficiency in volunteer supervision, are much more meaningful indicators than certificates handed to staff on an annual basis, and staff will be well aware of the difference.

HERE ARE SOME SPECIFIC TIPS:

Support the initial decision to employ volunteers:

◆ Attempt to reduce staff anxiety by indicating that the decision is under their control at all times.

◆ Follow-up both by telephone calls and face-to-face to discuss potential problems.

◆ Ask for feedback, both positive and negative.

◆ Introduce staff to other volunteer users. Build a support network.

Help manage the implementation:

◆ Keep in touch, and keep staff informed on progress or lack of it.

◆ Assist staff with getting the decision to use volunteers approved.

◆ Assist staff with paperwork.

◆ Involve staff in recruitment, interviewing, induction, etc.

◆ Advise staff of key management requirements.

Enhance the relationship:

◆ Be available.

◆ Arrange for continual personal communication.

◆ Do not wait for staff to come to you - check for problems by approaching them.

◆ Facilitate open, candid communication.

◆ Maintain high quality volunteer referrals.

◆ Become a resource for information, help, new ideas, problem solving.

◆ Praise staff for good work, and inform their line manager.

Deal with dissatisfaction:

◆ Empathise with staff feelings.

◆ Respond to problems promptly.

◆ Continue to anticipate concerns and expectations.

◆ Reinforce the anticipated benefits.

◆ Never attempt to force continuing use of volunteers if things are not working out – withdraw the volunteers and deal with the problem, then seek to re-introduce usage.

CREATING SENIOR MANAGEMENT SUPPORT

Senior management must not only endorse the use of volunteers in the organisation but must also endorse the overall concept of a volunteer programme.

❶ Understanding

Obtaining a firm commitment from senior management first requires that they actually understand the nature of the volunteer programme.

This requires that they themselves know why they wish to have volunteers connected with the organisation. Senior management must be happy with their decision to introduce a volunteer programme, and recognise that the volunteers have the ability to contribute to the success of the organisation.

Their decision should be based on whatever rationale they choose to adopt, whether viewing volunteers as a source of community input or community outreach, or simply viewing volunteers as a cost-effective method of service delivery. The particular rationale is not as important as the fact that there is *some* commonly accepted rationale. If there is not one, you would be wise to lead senior staff through a planning exercise to formulate one. If you do not do this, you risk having several different, and perhaps mutually exclusive, opinions of why the volunteer programme should exist, or risk the prospect that no one in senior management really understands why it does exist. It is difficult to fully support something which you do not fully understand, particularly in a budget crisis.

Linked to this rationale is a second requirement, that senior management understand what needs to be done to establish and resource an effective volunteer programme. They must have an understanding of the volunteer management process and the investment needed to make effective use of volunteers.

❷ Information

Senior management support will require sufficient information to judge whether the volunteer programme is successful.

This information can take a number of forms:

KEYS TO MANAGEMENT SUPPORT

There are three elements which are essential in gaining support from senior management.

❶ Understanding

Senior management must understand the volunteer programme in terms of what it aims to achieve and how it operates, including the relationship of the volunteers to the staff.

❷ Information

Senior management must understand what the volunteer programme can accomplish compared with the financial and personnel costs required to run the programme, and must understand that the benefits outweigh the costs.

❸ Involvement

Senior management must understand what they can and should do to assist the volunteer programme.

Patterns of volunteer use

This might consist of reports on where and how volunteers are being deployed. A report would include, for example, a department-by-department listing of how many volunteers are involved, how many hours they are contributing, and what types of jobs they are doing. The value of this type of report is that it allows senior management to identify patterns of usage, highlighting staff and departments who are doing a particularly good job of involving volunteers and those who are not.

It also shows senior management the types of work that volunteers are capable of doing.

Value of the volunteers

It is valuable to include estimates of the value to the organisation of the volunteer contribution. This would include tracking a number of items:

◆ Value of donated volunteer time: calculating the number of volunteer hours and multiplying it by an estimated hourly wage. This estimated wage can be derived from a statistical estimate of what volunteers would otherwise earn with their time in their occupations (about $11 per hour in the US and £4 in the UK), or by a calculated figure for each particular volunteer job (for example, a legal advisor would be valued at a much higher hourly rate than a general dogsbody).

◆ Value of in-kind donations made by volunteers: recording the value of any personal or business equipment donated by the volunteer, including use of business office space or other facilities, personal equipment, etc.

◆ Direct cash donations by volunteers: tracking any direct donations made by volunteers. Studies have shown that volunteers are much more likely than any other group to make a donation – although some organisations have a policy of not approaching their volunteers for cash support. Another measure might be legacy pledges.

◆ Un-reimbursed volunteer expenses: recording the expenses incurred by volunteers (mileage, phone calls, copying, etc.) for which they have not sought organisation reimbursement. Some organisations have a policy of encouraging reimbursement of all volunteer expenses, but then providing a system for the re-donation of such expenses back to the organisation.

Information should be provided to senior management in a combination of facts (statistics, lists, etc.) and stories (anecdotes, case studies, interesting personalities or snippets of information, etc.)

❸ Involvement

The final element of senior management support involves telling them how and when they can be helpful to the programme.

There are several functions at which an appearance by senior management is extremely valuable. These include appearing at volunteer orientations, giving out volunteer recognition items, and meeting occasionally with groups of volunteers. It also includes being generally supportive on an on-going basis. One excellent example of top management support occurs in a hospital whose chief administrator has an hourly meeting with volunteers each Tuesday, rotating the invitees among the volunteers in various departments. Another hospital administrator memorises names and photographs of new volunteers, and then 'casually' greets them in the halls of the hospital, welcoming them on behalf of the institution.

Senior managers also have roles to play in encouraging staff to value the volunteer input, to reward staff who work well with volunteers, and to convince other staff that they should do better.

Perhaps the best encouragement that senior management can provide staff is through example. If the top management make effective use of volunteers, other staff will receive a clear message regarding the value and importance of volunteers to the organisation.

THE FUTURE

In an absolute sense, it is difficult to draw any clear philosophical distinction between what is inherently a 'staff' function and what is a 'volunteer' function. Different organisations will reach very different conclusions about appropriate patterns of work, based on philosophy, history, contractual agreements, etc.

It is also difficult to contemplate some of the possible managerial implications for the more creative arrangements which are now being experimented with. In the US, as an example, the American National Red Cross has been contemplating implications of their staffing patterns, which consist of paired teams of volunteers and staff at all levels, and in which volunteers exercise supervisory responsibility over paid staff. Here are some of the resultant managerial recommendations from their *Volunteer 2000* report:

CASE STUDY

THE AMERICAN NATIONAL RED CROSS
MANAGERIAL RECOMMENDATIONS

It is recommended that the degree of volunteer involvement in a unit or service not be measured by absolute increases or decreases in volunteer numbers, but rather by the degree of volunteer intensiveness, i.e. the ratio between volunteer and paid staff.

It is recommended that training in volunteer administration and/or substantial experience in volunteer administration be a prerequisite for being hired into a Red Cross human resources management position.

It is recommended that where paid staff/volunteer teams exist, performance evaluation occur on a team basis rather than one team member evaluating the other. The evaluation of team relationships should take place in one of two ways:

◆ The team is evaluated as a unit, and both partners share responsibility for the achievement of the entire spectrum of the unit's performance goals regardless of how they did, in fact, split the work load between them. In this method, the person or team at the next level reviews progress and adequacy of support levels with both team members simultaneously and in the presence of both.

◆ The partners are reviewed as individuals, each having negotiated separate performance goals and levels of support which, taken together, are the performance standards for the team. These performance and support goals for each partner would be negotiated initially between them, then in conference with the next higher level. The performance appraisal would be done by the next higher level.

It is recommended that individual performance standards for paid and volunteer leadership staff always include as measures the degree of success demonstrated by that individual in recruiting and developing qualified volunteers for established volunteer positions, the degree of success in finding new ways of involving volunteers, and the degree of success in nominating appropriately qualified volunteers for awards and beyond-the-chapter positions.

The case study recommendations clearly envision a partnership in which the key factor is not that of who is paid and who is not, but rather how well the work is accomplished.

KEY POINTS

Follow these three general principles in planning your work with staff:

♦ Try to spend at least as much time working with staff as you do working directly with your volunteers. In the initial development of your programme plan to spend much more time with the staff.

♦ Deal with problems that arise as quickly as possible. Do not let a situation fester. And do not attempt to force people to get along. It is better for the volunteer to be transferred elsewhere than for you to try to enforce compatibility.

♦ Your ultimate objective is to get the staff to do the core work of volunteer management. If you can enable staff to become effective volunteer managers then you will be able to spend your time working on creative job development and troubleshooting. If you are forced to attempt to supervise all of the volunteers in the organisation, then you will be overwhelmed by the trivial.

CHAPTER TEN
SOME FINAL SUGGESTIONS

FINDING AN OVERALL APPROACH

In tackling the work outlined in the previous chapters it is essential to employ a coherent philosophical approach. Our suggestion for this approach would be to have you concentrate on two theories, which we think will make success more probable:

Start small, and grow with success

Do not expect to accomplish everything at once, and do not try to do so. Operating a volunteer programme is a delicate and complicated task, made so in part by the fact that the more successful you are at some things (such as recruitment), then the more work you will create for yourself. It is better to begin with little things and then grow a bit at a time, than to become over-extended and create bad feelings with unsuccessful volunteer placements. Happy staff and happy volunteers will become your best salespeople for the programme, but you have to make sure everyone is happy.

One way to start small is to begin with an ad hoc effort, a programme intended to make use of volunteers to accomplish just one thing. This will allow you to test the use of volunteers and identify the strengths and weaknesses that the organisation brings to involving volunteers.

Rely on persuasion, not coercion

Do not try to force volunteers on the organisation or on any member of staff. The use of volunteers will help the organisation, but only if a positive approach is adopted. Rely on the persuasion that is created by competence and success – if staff realise that some departments are gaining benefits through the use of volunteers then eventually they will decide to seek the same advantages for themselves. Have confidence in the value of volunteers, and be willing to let staff come to you, rather than feeling compelled to beg them. Never be foolish enough to believe that you can coerce anyone into using volunteers. A well-operated small volunteer programme is much more valuable then an ineffective large one.

Do not be afraid to make staff 'earn' the right to have volunteers assigned to them. This will help to convince staff that volunteers

> **Start small, and grow with success**

are not a 'free' resource, and will demonstrate that the organisation considers volunteers too valuable to be distributed to those who are not willing to make effective use of them.

THE GEOMETRY OF VOLUNTEER INVOLVEMENT

As you think about operating the programme, try to keep in mind the simple geometric shapes:

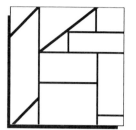

The Puzzle Square

representing the jobs which the organisation needs doing.

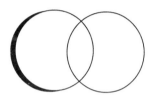

The Overlapping Circles

representing the commonly met needs of the organisation and the volunteers.

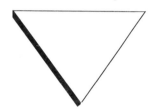

The Triangle

representing the web of relationships among the volunteer manager, and staff.

If you can construct a volunteer programme which embodies these shapes, you will have created a mechanism for effectively using volunteer resources.

THE GOLDEN RULE

Finally, remember the 'Golden Rule' of volunteer management:

 Their niceness will let you recruit a volunteer the first time, but only your competence will let you keep them

SAMPLE POLICY ON VOLUNTEER MANAGEMENT

This sample policy on volunteer management includes many of the ideas for good volunteer involvement expressed in this book. Not every item will be appropriate for every organisation, nor will the specific policy items suggested necessarily conform with how the organisation wishes to work with its volunteers. The sample policy is included more as a structure to help you construct your own policy on volunteer management which matches your views and needs, and which is appropriate to the size of your organisation and the ways in which you use your volunteers. To construct such a policy you may remove or amend any item, or even add further items not included here.

THE VOLUNTEER PROGRAMME

1.1 Overall policy on use of volunteers

The achievement of the goals of this organisation is best served by the active participation of citizens of the community. To this end, the organisation accepts and encourages the involvement of volunteers at all levels in the organisation and within all appropriate programmes and activities. All staff are encouraged to assist in the creation of meaningful and productive roles in which volunteers might serve and to assist in recruitment of volunteers from the community.

1.2 Purpose of the volunteer policy

The purpose of the policy is to provide overall guidance and direction to staff and volunteers engaged in volunteer involvement and management efforts. The policy is intended for internal management guidance only, and does not constitute, either implicitly or explicitly, a binding contractual or personnel agreement. The organisation reserves the exclusive right to change any aspect of the policy at any time and to expect adherence to the changed policy. Alterations to or exceptions from the policy may only be granted by the volunteer programme manager, and must be obtained in advance and in writing. Matters in areas not specifically covered by the policy shall be decided by the volunteer programme manager.

1.3 Scope of the volunteer policy

Unless specifically stated, the policy applies to all non-elected volunteers in all programmes and projects undertaken by or on behalf of the organisation, and to all departments and sites of operation of the organisation.

1.4 Role of the volunteer management department

The productive use of volunteers requires a planned and organised effort. The function of the volunteer management department is to provide a central coordinating point for effective volunteer management within the organisation, and to direct and assist staff and volunteer efforts jointly to provide more productive services. The department shall also bear responsibility for maintaining liaison with other volunteer programmes in the community and assisting in community-wide efforts to recognise and promote volunteering. The volunteer programme manager shall bear primary responsibility for planning for effective volunteer deployment, for assisting staff in identifying productive and creative volunteer roles, for recruiting suitable volunteers, and for tracking and evaluating the contribution of volunteers to the organisation.

1.5 Definition of 'volunteer'

A 'volunteer' is anyone who without compensation or expectation of compensation beyond reimbursement of expenses incurred in the course of his or her volunteer duties performs a task at the direction of and on behalf of the organisation. A 'volunteer' must be officially accepted and enrolled by the organisation prior to performance of the task. Unless specifically stated, volunteers shall not be considered as 'employees' of the organisation.

1.6 Special case volunteers

The organisation also accepts as volunteers those participating in student community service activities, student intern projects, alternative sentencing programmes, employee volunteering programmes, and other volunteer referral programmes. In each of these cases, however, a special agreement must be in effect with the agency, school, company, or programme from which the special case volunteers originate and must identify responsibility for management and care of the volunteers.

1.7 Employees as volunteers

The organisation accepts [*does not accept*] the services of its own staff as volunteers. This service is accepted provided that the volunteer service is provided totally without any coercive nature, involves work which is outside the scope of normal staff duties, and is provided outside usual working hours. Family members of staff are [*are not*] allowed to volunteer with the organisation. When family members are enrolled as volunteers, they will not be placed under the direct supervision or within the same department as other members of their family who are employees.

1.8 Clients and relatives as volunteers

Clients of the organisation may be accepted as volunteers, where such service does not constitute an obstruction to or conflict with provision of services to the client or to others. Relatives of clients may also serve as volunteers, but will not be placed in a position of direct service or relationship to members of their family who are receiving services.

1.9 Service at the discretion of the organisation

The organisation accepts the service of all volunteers with the understanding that such service is at the sole discretion of the organisation. Volunteers agree that the organisation may at any time, for whatever reason, decide to terminate the volunteer's relationship with the organisation.

A volunteer may at any time, for whatever reason, decide to sever the volunteer's relationship with the organisation. Notice of such a decision should be communicated as soon as possible to the volunteer's supervisor.

1.10 Volunteer rights and responsibilities

Volunteers are viewed as a valuable resource to this organisation, its staff, and its clients. Volunteers shall be extended the right to be given meaningful assignments, the right to be treated as equal co-workers, the right to effective supervision, the right to full involvement and participation, and the right to recognition for work done. In return, volunteers shall agree to actively perform their duties to the best of their abilities and to remain loyal to the values, goals and procedures of the organisation.

1.11 Scope of volunteer involvement

Volunteers may be involved in all programmes and activities of the organisation, and serve at all levels of skill and decision-making. Volunteers should not, however, be used to displace any paid employees from their positions.

VOLUNTEER MANAGEMENT PROCEDURES

2.1 Maintenance of records

A system of records will be maintained on each volunteer, including dates of service, positions held, duties performed, evaluation of work, and awards received. Volunteers and appropriate staff shall be responsible for submitting all appropriate records and information to the volunteer management department in a timely and accurate fashion.

Volunteer personnel records shall be accorded the same confidentiality as staff personnel records.

2.2 Two hat policy

Members of the organisation's management committee are [are not] accepted as direct service volunteers with the organisation.

2.3 Conflict of interest

No person who has a conflict of interest with any activity or programme of the organisation, whether personal, philosophical, or financial shall be accepted to serve as a volunteer.

2.4 Representation of the organisation

Prior to any action or statement which might significantly affect or obligate the organisation, volunteers should seek prior consultation and approval from appropriate staff. These actions may include, but are not limited to, public statements to the press, lobbying efforts with other organisations, collaborations or joint initiatives, or any agreements involving contractual or other financial obligations. Volunteers are authorised to act as representatives of the organisation as specifically indicated within their job descriptions and only to the extent of such written specifications.

2.5 Confidentiality

Volunteers are responsible for maintaining the confidentiality of all proprietary or privileged information to which they are exposed while serving as a volunteer, whether this information involves a single member of staff, volunteer, client, or other person or involves the overall business of the organisation.

Failure to maintain confidentiality may result in termination of the volunteer's relationship with the organisation or other corrective action.

2.6 Worksite

An appropriate worksite shall be established prior to the enrolment of any volunteer. This worksite shall contain necessary facilities, equipment, and space to enable the volunteer to perform his or her duties effectively and comfortably.

2.7 Dress code

As representatives of the organisation, volunteers, like staff, are responsible for presenting a good image to clients and to the community. Volunteers shall dress appropriately for the conditions and performance of their duties.

2.8 Timesheets

Individual volunteers are responsible for the accurate completion and timely submission of timesheets.

VOLUNTEER RECRUITMENT & SELECTION

3.1 Position descriptions

Volunteer staff, just as paid staff, require a clear, complete, and current description of the duties and responsibilities of the position which they are expected to fill. Prior to any volunteer assignment or recruitment effort, a position description must be developed for each volunteer post. This will be given to each accepted volunteer and used in subsequent management and evaluation efforts. Position descriptions should be reviewed and updated at least every two years, or whenever the work involved in the position changes substantially.

All position descriptions shall include a description of the purpose and duties of the position, a designated supervisor and worksite, a timeframe for the performance of the job, a listing of job qualifications, and a description of job benefits. The volunteer management department is available to assist staff in the development of volunteer jobs and position descriptions.

3.2 Staff requests for volunteers

Requests for volunteers shall be submitted in writing by interested staff, complete with a draft position description and a requested timeframe. All parties should understand that the recruitment of volunteers is enhanced by creative and interesting jobs and by advance notice. The volunteer management department reserves the right to refuse to recruit or place any volunteers until staff are prepared to make effective use of the volunteer resource.

3.3 Recruitment

Volunteers shall be recruited by the organisation on a pro-active basis, with the intent of broadening and expanding the volunteer involvement of the community. Volunteers shall be recruited without regard to gender, disability, age, race or other condition. The sole qualification for volunteer recruitment shall be suitability to perform a task on behalf of the organisation. Volunteers may be recruited either through an interest in specific functions or through a general interest in volunteering which will later be matched with a specific function. No final acceptance of a volunteer shall take place without a specific written volunteer position description for that volunteer.

3.4 Recruitment of minors

Volunteers who have not reached the age of majority must have the written consent of a parent or guardian prior to volunteering. The volunteer services assigned to a minor should be performed in a non-hazardous environment and should comply with all appropriate requirements of child labour laws.

3.5 Interviewing

Prior to being assigned or appointed to a position, all volunteers will be interviewed to ascertain their suitability for and interest in that position. The interview should determine the qualifications of the volunteer, their commitment to fulfil the requirements of the position, and should answer any questions that the volunteer might have about the position. Interviews may be conducted either in person or by other means.

3.6 Health screening

In cases where volunteers will be working with clients with health difficulties, a health screening procedure may be required prior to confirming the volunteer assignment. In addition, if there are physical requirements necessary for performance of a task, a screening or testing procedure may be required to ascertain the ability of the volunteer to perform that task safely.

3.7 Criminal records check

As appropriate for the protection of clients, volunteers in certain assignments may be asked to submit to a background criminal record check. Volunteers who do not agree to the background check may be refused the assignment.

3.8 Placement with at-risk clients

Where volunteers are to be placed in direct contact with at-risk clients, additional screening procedures may be instituted. These procedures may include reference checks, direct background investigation, criminal investigation, etc. Volunteers who refuse permission for conduct of these checks will not be accepted for placement with clients.

3.9 Certificate of ability

Any potential volunteer who indicates that they are under the care of a doctor for either physical or psychological treatment may be asked to present a certificate from the doctor as to their ability to perform their volunteer duties satisfactorily and safely. Volunteers under a course of treatment which might affect their volunteer work will not be accepted without written verification of suitability from their doctor. Any volunteer who, after acceptance and assignment by the organisation, enters a course of treatment which might adversely impact upon the performance of their volunteer duties should consult with the volunteer programme manager.

3.10 Placement

In placing a volunteer in a position, attention shall be paid to the interests and capabilities of the volunteer and to the requirements of the volunteer position. No placement shall be made unless the requirements of both the volunteer and the supervising staff can be met: no volunteer should be assigned to a 'make-work' position, and no position should be given to an unqualified or uninterested volunteer.

3.11 Staff participation in interviewing & placement

Wherever possible, staff who will be working with the volunteer should participate in the design and conduct of the interview. Final assignment of a potential volunteer should not take place without the approval of appropriate staff with whom the volunteer will be working.

3.12 Acceptance & appointment

Service as a volunteer with the organisation shall begin with an official notice of acceptance or appointment to a volunteer position. Notice may only be given by an authorised representative of the organisation, who will normally be the volunteer programme manager. No volunteer shall begin performance of any position until they have been officially accepted for that position and have completed all necessary screening and paperwork. At the time of final acceptance, each volunteer shall complete all necessary enrolment paperwork and shall receive a copy of their job description and agreement of service with the organisation.

3.13 Probationary period

All volunteer placements shall initially be done on a trial period of 30 days. At the end of this period a second interview with the volunteer shall be conducted, at which point either the volunteer or staff may request a re-assignment of the volunteer to a different position or may determine the unsuitability of the volunteer for a position within the organisation.

3.14 Re-assignment

Volunteers who are at any time re-assigned to a new position shall be interviewed for that position and shall receive all appropriate orientation and training for that position before they begin work. In addition, any screening procedures appropriate for that specific position must be completed, even if the volunteer has already been working with the organisation.

3.15 Professional services

Volunteers shall not perform professional services for which certification or a licence is required unless currently certified or licensed to do so. A copy of such a certificate or licence should be maintained by the volunteer management department.

3.16 Length of service

All volunteer positions shall have a set term of duration. It is highly recommended that this term shall not be longer than one-year, with an option for renewal at the discretion of both parties. All volunteer assignments shall end at the conclusion of their set term, without expectation or requirement of re-assignment of that position to the incumbent.

Volunteers are neither expected nor required to continue their involvement with the organisation at the end of the set term, although in most cases they are welcome to do so. They may instead seek a different volunteer assignment within the organisation or with another organisation, or may retire from volunteer service.

3.17 Leave of absence

At the discretion of the supervisor, leave of absence may be granted to volunteers. This leave of absence will not alter or extend the previously agreed upon ending date of the volunteer's term of service.

VOLUNTEER TRAINING & DEVELOPMENT

4.1 Orientation

All volunteers will receive a general orientation on the nature and purpose of the organisation, an orientation on the nature and operation of the programme or activity for which they are recruited, and a specific orientation on the purposes and requirements of the position which they are accepting.

4.2 On-the-job training

Volunteers will receive specific on-the-job training to provide them with the information and skills necessary to perform their volunteer assignment. The timing and methods for delivery of such training should be appropriate to the complexity and demands of the position and the capabilities of the volunteer.

4.3 Staff involvement in orientation and training

Staff members with responsibility for delivery of services should have an active role in the design and delivery of both orientation and training of volunteers. Staff who will be in a supervisory capacity to volunteers shall have primary responsibility for design and delivery of on-the-job training to those volunteers assigned to them.

4.4 Volunteer involvement in orientation and training

Experienced volunteers should be included in the design and delivery of volunteer orientation and training.

4.5 Continuing education

Just as with staff, volunteers should attempt to improve their levels of skill during their terms of service. Additional training and educational opportunities will be made available to volunteers during their connection with the organisation where deemed appropriate. This continuing education may include both additional information on performance of their current volunteer assignment as well as more general information, and might be provided either by the organisation or by assisting the volunteer to participate in educational programmes provided by other groups.

4.6 Conference attendance

Volunteers are authorised to attend conferences and meetings which are relevant to their volunteer assignments, including those run by the organisation and those run by other organisations. Prior approval from the volunteer's supervisor should be obtained before attending any conference or meeting if attendance will interfere with the volunteer's work schedule, or if reimbursement of expenses is sought.

VOLUNTEER SUPERVISION & EVALUATION

5.1 Requirement of a supervisor

Each volunteer who is accepted to a position with the organisation must have a clearly identified supervisor who is responsible for direct management of that volunteer. This supervisor shall be responsible for day-to-day management and guidance of the work of the volunteer, and shall be available to the volunteer for consultation and assistance.

5.2 Volunteers as volunteer supervisors

A volunteer may act as a supervisor of other volunteers, provided that the supervising volunteer is under the direct supervision of a paid member of staff .

5.3 Volunteer-staff relationships

Volunteers and staff are considered to be partners in implementing the mission and programmes of the organisation, with each having an equal but complementary role to play. It is essential in the proper operation of this relationship that each partner understand and respect the needs and abilities of the other.

5.4 Acceptance of volunteers by staff

Since individual members of staff are in a better position to determine the requirements of their work and their own abilities, no volunteer will be assigned to work with a member of staff without the consent of that person. Since volunteers are considered a valuable resource in performing the organisation's work, staff are encouraged to consider creative ways in which volunteers might be of service to the organisation and to consult with the volunteer management department if they feel in need of assistance or additional training.

5.5 Volunteer management training for members of staff

An orientation on working with volunteers will be provided to all staff. In-service training on effective volunteer deployment and use will be provided to those staff who are highly involved in volunteer management.

5.6 Volunteer involvement in staff evaluation

Examination of their effective use of volunteers may be a component in the evaluation of staff performance where that member of staff is working with volunteers. In such cases, supervisors should ask for the input and participation of those volunteers in evaluating staff performance.

5.7 Staff involvement in volunteer evaluation

Affected staff should be involved in all evaluation and in deciding all work assignments of volunteers with whom they are working.

5.8 Lines of communication

Volunteers are entitled to all necessary information pertinent to the performance of their work assignments. Accordingly, volunteers should be included in and have access to all appropriate information, memos, materials, and meetings relevant to the work assignments. To facilitate the receipt of this information on a timely basis, volunteers should be included on all relevant distribution schedules and should be given a tray for receipt of information circulated in their absence. Primary responsibility for ensuring that the volunteer receives such information will rest with the direct supervisor of the volunteer.

Lines of communication should operate in both directions, and should exist both formally and informally. Volunteers should be consulted regarding all decisions which would substantially affect the performance of their duties.

5.9 Absenteeism

Volunteers are expected to perform their duties on a regular scheduled and punctual basis. When expecting to be absent from a scheduled duty, volunteers should inform their staff supervisor as far in advance as possible so that alternative arrangements may be made. Continual absenteeism will result in a review of the volunteer's work assignment or term of service.

5.10 Substitution

Volunteers may be encouraged to find a substitute for any future absences which could be filled by another volunteer. Such substitution should only be taken following consultation with a supervisor, and care should be taken to find a substitute who is qualified for the position. Substitutes may only be recruited from those who are currently enrolled as volunteers with the organisation.

5.11 Standards of performance

Standards of performance shall be established for each volunteer position. These standards should list the work to be done in that position, measurable indicators of whether the work was accomplished to the required standards, and appropriate timeframes for accomplishment of the work. Creation of these standards will be a joint function of staff and the volunteer assigned to the position, and a copy of the standards should be provided to the volunteer along with a copy of their job description at the beginning of their assignment.

5.12 Evaluations

Volunteers shall receive periodic evaluation to review their work. The evaluation session will review the performance of the volunteer, suggest any changes in work style, seek suggestions from the volunteer on means of enhancing the volunteer's relationship with the organisation, convey appreciation to the volunteer, and ascertain the continued interest of the volunteer in serving in that position. Evaluations should include both an examination of the volunteer's performance of his or her responsibilities and a discussion of any suggestions that the volunteer may have concerning the position or project with which the volunteer is connected.

The evaluation session is an opportunity for both the volunteer and the organisation to examine and improve their relationship.

5.13 Written basis for evaluation

The position description and standards of performance for a volunteer position should form the basis of an evaluation. A written record should be kept of each evaluation session.

5.14 Staff responsibility for evaluation

It shall be the responsibility of each member of staff in a supervisory relationship with a volunteer to schedule and perform periodic evaluation and to maintain records of the evaluation.

5.15 Corrective action

In appropriate situations, corrective action may be taken following an evaluation. Examples of corrective action include the requirement for additional training, re-assignment of the volunteer to a new position, suspension of the volunteer, or dismissal from volunteer service.

5.16 Dismissal of a volunteer

Volunteers who do not adhere to the rules and procedures of the organisation or who fail satisfactorily to perform their volunteer assignment may be subject to dismissal. No volunteer will be terminated until the volunteer has had an opportunity to discuss the reasons for possible dismissal with supervisory staff. Prior to dismissal of a volunteer, any affected member of staff should seek the consultation and assistance of the volunteer programme manager.

5.17 Reasons for dismissal

Possible grounds for dismissal may include, but are not limited to, the following: gross misconduct or insubordination, being under the influence of alcohol or drugs, theft of property or misuse of organisation equipment or materials, abuse or mistreatment of clients or co-workers, failure to abide by organisation policies and procedures, failure to meet physical or mental standards of performance, and failure to perform assigned duties satisfactorily.

5.18 Concerns and grievances

Decisions involving corrective action of a volunteer may be reviewed for appropriateness. If corrective action is taken, the affected volunteer shall be informed of the procedures for expressing their concern or grievance.

5.19 Notice of departure or re-assignment of a volunteer

In the event that a volunteer departs from the organisation, whether voluntarily or involuntarily, or is re-assigned to a new position, it shall be the responsibility of the volunteer management department to inform those affected staff and clients that the volunteer is no longer assigned to work with them. In cases of dismissal for good reason, this notification should be given in writing and should clearly indicate that any further contact with the volunteer must be outside the scope of any relationship with the organisation.

5.20 Resignation

Volunteers may resign from their volunteer service with the organisation at any time. It is requested that volunteers who intend to resign provide advance notice of their departure and a reason for their decision.

5.21 Exit interviews

Exit interviews, where possible, should be conducted with volunteers who are leaving their positions. The interview should ascertain why the volunteer is leaving the position, suggestions the volunteer may have to improving the position, and the possibility of involving the volunteer in some other capacity with the organisation in the future.

5.22 Communication with the volunteer management department

Staff supervising volunteers are responsible for maintaining regular communication with the volunteer management department on the status of the volunteers they are supervising, and are responsible for the timely provision of all necessary paperwork to the department. The department should be informed immediately of any substantial change in the work or status of a volunteer, and should be consulted in advance before any corrective action is taken.

5.23 Evaluation of the organisation's volunteer usage

The volunteer management department shall conduct an annual evaluation of the use of volunteers by the organisation. This evaluation will include information gathered from volunteers, staff, and clients.

VOLUNTEER SUPPORT & RECOGNITION

6.1 Reimbursement of expenses

Volunteers are [*may be*] eligible for reimbursement of reasonable expenses incurred while undertaking business for the organisation. The volunteer management department shall distribute information to all volunteers regarding specific reimbursable items. Prior approval must be sought for any major expenditure.

6.2 Access to organisation property and materials

As appropriate, volunteers shall have access to property of the organisation and those materials necessary to fulfil their duties, and shall receive training in the operation of any equipment. Property and materials shall be used only when directly required for the volunteer task. This policy includes [*does not include*] access to and use of organisation vehicles.

6.3 Insurance

Liability and accident insurance is [*is not*] provided for all volunteers engaged in the organisation's business. [*Volunteers are encouraged to consult with their own insurance agents regarding the extension of their personal insurance to include community volunteer work. Specific information regarding such insurance is available from the volunteer management department.*]

6.4 Recognition

An annual volunteer recognition event will be conducted to highlight and reward the contribution of volunteers to the organisation. Volunteers will be consulted and involved in order to develop an appropriate format for the event.

6.5 Informal recognition

All staff and volunteers responsible for volunteer supervision are encouraged to undertake methods of recognition of volunteer service on a regular basis throughout the year. These methods of informal recognition should range from simple 'Thank You's' to a concerted effort to include volunteers as full participants in decision making and implementation for projects which involve the volunteer.

6.6 Volunteer career paths

Volunteers are encouraged to develop their skills while serving with the organisation, and are to be assisted through promotion to new volunteer jobs to assume additional and greater responsibilities. If so desired by the volunteer, the organisation will assist the volunteer in maintaining appropriate records of volunteer experience that will assist the volunteer in future career opportunities, both paid and volunteer.

6.7 Staff recognition

The volunteer management department shall design a recognition programme for staff who work well with volunteers, and shall consult with volunteers to identify appropriate staff to receive such awards.

A selection of forms you might use or adapt for your organisation:

◆

Staff assessment survey on volunteer involvement

◆

Staff request form for volunteer assistance

◆

Volunteer position description

◆

Volunteer enrolment form

◆

Volunteer interview record

◆

Volunteer agreement

◆

Volunteer assignment log

◆

Volunteer time sheet

◆

Volunteer expenses claim form

◆

Volunteer contributions record

◆

Staff assessment of volunteer use

◆

Volunteer assessment of the volunteer programme

◆

Volunteer evaluation form

◆

Exit interview questionnaire

STAFF ASSESSMENT SURVEY ON VOLUNTEER INVOLVEMENT

As part of our plan to encourage volunteer assistance, we would like you to complete the following questionnaire. This survey is designed to help us assess our readiness to use volunteers and to determine what we need to do to ensure continued delivery of high quality services to our clients. All of the information collected will be kept confidential.

Experience with Volunteers

1. Have you previously worked in an organisation which used volunteers?
   ❑ Yes ❑ No ❑ Don't Know

2. Have you previously supervised any volunteers?
   ❑ Yes ❑ No ❑ Don't Know

3. Do you do volunteer work yourself?
   ❑ Yes ❑ No ❑ Once did, but not any more.

Assessment of Volunteer Involvement

1. What is your overall assessment of the desirability of using volunteers in our organisation at this time?
   ❑ Very desirable   ❑ Somewhat desirable
   ❑ Uncertain   ❑ Not desirable at this time ❑ Would never be appropriate

2. What is your overall assessment of our organisation's current ability to work with volunteers?
   ❑ Very able   ❑ Somewhat able   ❑ Uncertain   ❑ Not able

3. Are there any areas or types of work for which you think that volunteers are particularly needed and suited?

4. Are there any areas or types of work which you think volunteers should not do?

5. What issues or concerns would you like to see addressed before we use volunteers?

6. What type of training or help would you like to receive before you are asked to work with volunteers?

7. Are there any other comments, concerns, or questions that you would like to express about the involvement of volunteers in our agency?

Please return this questionnaire to _____   by _____

STAFF REQUEST FORM FOR VOLUNTEER ASSISTANCE

Date of Request _____ Department _____

Staff Contact _____ Phone _____

Brief Description of Work to be Performed

Give both goal of the job and examples of activities to be performed:

_____

_____

_____

Qualifications Sought

Include both skills and attributes needed to perform the work, and any items that might disqualify an applicant:

_____

_____

_____

WORKSITE: _____

TIMEFRAME: _____

HOURS PREFERRED:
- ❑ Flexible to availability of volunteer   ❑ Required:

LENGTH OF COMMITMENT SOUGHT:
- ❑ Open-ended   ❑ Minimum of:
- ❑ Fixed period:

When do you want this job to start?
- ❑ Upon availability   ❑ Start date:

NUMBER OF VOLUNTEERS SOUGHT FOR THIS POSITION: _____

Please return this form to:

Name: _____

Address: _____

We will be happy to work with you in completing this form. Call us at _____ if you would like assistance in developing new volunteer jobs or in learning more about working effectively with volunteers.

VOLUNTEER POSITION DESCRIPTION

Title/Position: _____

Goal of Position: _____

Sample Activities:

    1. _____

    2. _____

    3. _____

    4. _____

Timeframe:

Length of commitment: _____

Estimated total hours: _____

Scheduling:

    ❑ At discretion of volunteer

    ❑ Required: _____

Worksite: _____
_____

Qualifications Sought:

    1. _____

    2. _____

    3. _____

    4. _____

Benefits to the Volunteer:

    1. _____

    2. _____

For further information:

Contact: _____

Phone: _____ Date: _____

VOLUNTEER ENROLMENT FORM

Name: _____ Phone: (H) _____ (O) _____

Address: _____

Contact in Emergency: Name: _____ Phone: _____

Skills and Interests

Educational Background: _____

Current Occupation: _____

Hobbies, Interests, Skills: _____

Previous Volunteer Experience: _____

IS THERE A PARTICULAR TYPE OF VOLUNTEER WORK IN WHICH YOU ARE INTERESTED? *(Tick all that apply)*

- ❑ No preference
- ❑ Working directly with a member of staff as an assistant
- ❑ Helping in general administrative duties
- ❑ Fundraising
- ❑ Doing research, teaching, or an individual project
- ❑ Working one-on-one with a single client
- ❑ Providing a service to several clients
- ❑ Public speaking
- ❑ Editing the newsletter
- ❑ Other: _____

IS THERE A CLIENT OR GROUP WITH WHOM YOU ARE PARTICULARLY INTERESTED IN WORKING? *(Tick all that apply)*

- ❑ Adults
- ❑ Elderly
- ❑ Teens
- ❑ Children
- ❑ Handicapped
- ❑ Males
- ❑ Females
- ❑ No Preference
- ❑ Other: _____
- ❑ Not interested in working with clients

ARE THERE ANY GROUPS YOU WOULD NOT FEEL COMFORTABLE WORKING WITH?

- ❑ No
- ❑ Yes: _____

Availability

AT WHAT TIMES ARE YOU INTERESTED IN VOLUNTEERING?

- ❑ Flexible
- ❑ Prefer weekdays
- ❑ Prefer evenings
- ❑ Prefer weekends
- ❑ Prefer daytime
- ❑ Other:
- ❑ There are times during a week that I cannot do volunteer work: _____

Do you have a geographic preference as to where you do volunteer work? ❑ No ❑ Yes: _____

Do you have access to a car you can use for volunteer work?   ❑ Yes ❑ No ❑ Occasionally

References

HOW DID YOU HEAR ABOUT US?
- ❑ Referred by a volunteer
- ❑ Volunteer Bureau
- ❑ Advertisement
- ❑ Referred by a friend
- ❑ From client of the organisation
- ❑ Other: _____

NAME AND PHONE NUMBERS OF TWO PERSONAL REFERENCES:

Name: _____ Phone: _____

Name: _____ Phone: _____

Please return this form to: _____

VOLUNTEER INTERVIEW RECORD

Interviewer: _____ Date: _____

Name of Volunteer: _____ Phone: _____

Review of Enrolment Form

Clarify information on Volunteer Enrolment Form. Correct information supplied on the form and place other comments below.

_____

Non-Directive Questions

1. What attracted you to our organisation? Is there any aspect of our work that most motivates you to volunteer here?

   _____

2. What would you like to get out of volunteering here? What would make you feel like you've been successful?

   _____

3. What have you enjoyed most about your previous volunteer work?

   _____

4. What have you previously enjoyed about your paid job?

   _____

5. How would you like to be supervised?

   _____

6. Would you rather work on your own, with a group, or with a partner? Why?

   _____

7. What skills do you feel you have to contribute?

   _____

8. What can I tell you about our organisation?

   _____

Match with Volunteer Positions

Discuss potential volunteer positions and check match of interests, qualifications, and availability.

   Position   Comments

1. _____

2. _____

3. _____

VOLUNTEER INTERVIEW RECORD

To be completed after interview.

Interviewer Assessment

APPEARANCE:

❑ Poised, neat ❑ Acceptable ❑ Unkempt

HEALTH AND PHYSICAL ABILITY: _____

_____

REACTIONS TO QUESTIONS:

❑ Helpful, interested, volunteers information ❑ Answers questions

❑ Evasive ❑ Confused

DISPOSITION:

❑ Outgoing, confident ❑ Reserved ❑ Pleasant

❑ Withdrawn, moody ❑ Suspicious, antagonistic ❑ Nothing remarkable

INTERPERSONAL SKILLS:

❑ Adept at dealing with others ❑ Relatively at ease with others ❑ Uncomfortable

Recommended Action

❑ Consider for following positions:

1. _____

2. _____

❑ Schedule for second interview.

❑ Hold in reserve for position of:

1. _____

2. _____

❑ Investigate further:

_____

❑ Refer to: _____

❑ Not suitable for organisation at this time.

Notification

❑ Volunteer notified of decision:

Name: _____

Date and method: _____

VOLUNTEER AGREEMENT

This agreement is intended to indicate the seriousness with which we treat our volunteers. The intention of the agreement is to assure you both of our deep appreciation of your services and to indicate our commitment to do the very best we can to make your volunteer experience here a productive and rewarding one.

The Organisation

We, ——————————————— (the organisation), agree to accept the services of

——————————————— (volunteer) beginning ———————————————,

and we commit to the following:

1. To provide adequate information, training, and assistance for the volunteer to be able to meet the responsibilities of their volunteer job.

2. To ensure satisfactory supervisory support to the volunteer and to provide feedback on performance.

3. To respect the skills, dignity and individual needs of the volunteer, and to do our best to adjust to these individual requirements.

4. To be receptive to any comments from the volunteer regarding ways in which we might mutually better accomplish our respective tasks.

5. To treat the volunteer as an equal partner with the organisation's staff, jointly responsible for completion of the organisation's goals and the fulfilment of its mission.

The Volunteer

Agrees to serve as a volunteer and commits to the following:

1. To perform my volunteer duties to the best of my ability.

2. To adhere to the organisation's rules and procedures, including record-keeping requirements and confidentiality of organisation and client information.

3. To meet time and duty commitments, except in exceptional circumstances, or to provide adequate notice so that alternate arrangements can be made.

Agreed to:

————————————————

Volunteer

————————————————

Date

————————————————

Staff Representative

————————————————

Date

This agreement may be cancelled at any time at the discretion of either of the parties, but will expire automatically on ——————————— unless renewed by both parties.

VOLUNTEER ASSIGNMENT LOG

Position (or department): _____ Month: _____

This is a multiple-use form for tracking volunteer assignments. If labeled by 'Month' in the upper right hand corner, the form becomes a month-by-month master list of all volunteers. If labeled 'Position', the sheet records all volunteers working in a particular job. If labeled 'Department,' the form records all volunteers assigned to that department.

NAME	DEPARTMENT	POSITION	STARTING DATE	ENDING DATE	NOTES
1.					
2.					
3.					
4.					
5.					
6.					
7.					
8.					
9.					
10.					
11.					
12.					
13.					
14.					
15.					
16.					
17.					
18.					
19.					
20.					
21.					
22.					
23.					
24.					

VOLUNTEER TIME SHEET

VOLUNTEER: MONTH:

Day	Department/Location	Job Assignment	Total Hours
1			
2			
3			
4			
5			
6			
7			
8			
9			
10			
11			
12			
13			
14			
15			
16			
17			
18			
19			
20			
21			
22			
23			
24			
25			
26			
26			
28			
29			
30			
31			
		TOTAL HOURS	

Please return this form by the 7th of the next month to:

VOLUNTEER EXPENSES CLAIM FORM

This form is to be used to record those expenses you incur while volunteering for us *for which you wish to be reimbursed.* The types of expenses for which we provide reimbursement are:

1. _____

2. _____

3. _____

4. _____

Month: _____

DATE	TYPE OF EXPENDITURE	AMOUNT
	TOTAL	

These represent an accurate account of my expenses.

_____

NAME OF VOLUNTEER

_____

DATE

Cash/Payment Received

_____

VOLUNTEER SIGNATURE

Approved for reimbursement.

_____

SUPERVISOR

_____

DATE

_____

PAYMENT ISSUED
For office use only

Please return this form by the 7th of the next month to:

_____

VOLUNTEER CONTRIBUTIONS RECORD

This form is to be used to record donations of money, in-kind contributions, and expenses incurred while volunteering for which you are not asking to be reimbursed.

Please complete the form and submit it to _____ so that we can use the information in our volunteering statistics to demonstrate the added value that our volunteers bring to the organisation. We promise confidentiality.

DATE	NATURE OF CONTRIBUTION	AMOUNT
	TOTAL	

I certify that these represent an accurate portrayal of my contributions:

_____

VOLUNTEER

_____

SIGNATURE

_____

DATE

STAFF ASSESSMENT OF VOLUNTEER USE

This form is to allow you to provide feedback regarding our organisation's use of volunteers. Please answer all questions as completely as possible. Do not sign the survey unless you wish to. All responses will be kept confidential.

1. Are volunteers involved in your area of direct responsibility or in your department?
   - ❑ Yes　　　❑ No　　　❑ Don't know

2. In your experience, are our volunteers adequately qualified for the work we ask them to do?
   - ❑ Yes　　　❑ No　　　❑ Don't know

3. How would you describe the use of volunteers by our staff?
   - ❑ Well used　　　❑ Generally well used, but some exceptions
   - ❑ Generally not well used　　　❑ Don't know

4. Are our volunteers adequately trained for their responsibilities?
   - ❑ Yes　　　❑ No　　　❑ Don't know

5. Do you think our staff has been adequately trained in how to work with volunteers?
   - ❑ Yes　　　❑ No　　　❑ Don't know

6. What else should be done to help our staff work better with volunteers?

   _____

7. How would you describe the reaction of our clients to our volunteers?
   - ❑ Favourable　　　❑ Mixed　　　❑ Unfavourable　　　❑ Don't know

8. What benefits do you think we have gained by using volunteers?

   _____

9. What problems have we created through the use of volunteers?

   _____

10. How has your own workload changed as a result of our using volunteers?
    - ❑ Lessened　　　❑ Remained the same　　　❑ Increased
    - ❑ Changed in type of work done

11. How would you describe the assistance you have received from the Volunteer Manager?
    - ❑ Helpful　　　❑ Not helpful　　　❑ Don't know

12. Use the space below to make any further comments regarding our use of volunteers, any additions you would like to make to your answers to the above questions, or any suggestions you have about how we might make better use of volunteers.

    _____

    _____

    _____

Please return this questionnaire to: _____ *by :* _____

VOLUNTEER ASSESSMENT OF THE VOLUNTEER PROGRAMME

As part of our continued effort to improve our volunteer programme, we would like your responses to the following questions. All responses will be kept completely confidential. Do not sign the survey unless you wish to.

1. How long have you been volunteering with us? _____

2. What is the best experience you have had while volunteering with us?

   _____

   What is the worst experience? _____

3. To what extent do you think our volunteers are accepted by the staff?
   - ❑ Well accepted ❑ Generally well accepted, but some exceptions
   - ❑ Mixed reception ❑ Generally not well accepted, but some exceptions ❑ Not well accepted

4. To what extent do you think volunteers are involved in reaching decisions that affect their volunteer work?
   - ❑ Well involved ❑ Sometimes involved ❑ Not well involved

5. To what extent do you think volunteers are accepted by clients?
   - ❑ Well accepted ❑ Mixed reception ❑ Not well accepted

6. To what extent do you think volunteers feel comfortable with the tasks they are given?
   - ❑ Comfortable ❑ Not very comfortable ❑ Don't know

7. Do you feel that volunteers receive sufficient induction to the organisation and its work when they start?
   - ❑ Yes ❑ No ❑ Don't know

8. Do you feel that volunteers receive enough training in how to carry out their assignments?
   - ❑ Yes ❑ No ❑ Don't know

9. In your experience, does your volunteer job match the description of work given to you when you were interviewed?
   - ❑ Yes ❑ Mostly ❑ No

10. Do you find your volunteer work interesting, challenging, and rewarding?
    - ❑ Yes ❑ Mostly ❑ No

    If you answered 'No,' do you have any comments on why that is?

11. Do you think that volunteers are provided with sufficient feedback by those they work with?
    - ❑ Yes ❑ More or less ❑ No ❑ Don't know

12. Do you think volunteers are given sufficient opportunity for increased responsibility in this organisation?
    - ❑ Yes ❑ No ❑ Don't know

15. Can you think of any new areas with which volunteers might be of help in our organisation?

    _____

16. Can you suggest any ways that we might use to recruit new volunteers?

    _____

17. Overall, how would you rate our volunteer programme? (Please circle. 1 = Terrible, 7 = Great)

    1   2   3   4   5   6   7

18. Use the space below to make any other comments regarding our organisation's use of volunteers, or any additions you would like to make to your answers to the above questions:

    _____

Please return this questionnaire to: _____ *by:* _____

VOLUNTEER EVALUATION FORM

NAME OF VOLUNTEER: _____   PERIOD COVERED BY EVALUATION:

POSITION: _____   DATE OF EVALUATION:

Position Goals

	NOT MET	SATISFACTORY		WELL MET	
1. _____	1	2	3	4	5
2. _____	1	2	3	4	5
3. _____	1	2	3	4	5
4. _____	1	2	3	4	5
5. _____	1	2	3	4	5

Work Relationships

	NEEDS IMPROVEMENT	SATISFACTORY		EXCELLENT	
1. Relations with other volunteers _____	1	2	3	4	5
2. Relations with staff _____	1	2	3	4	5
3. Relations with clients _____	1	2	3	4	5
4. Meeting commitments on hours and deadlines _____	1	2	3	4	5
5. Initiative _____	1	2	3	4	5
6. Flexibility _____	1	2	3	4	5

Comments by supervisor regarding above areas:

Comments by volunteer regarding above areas:

Overall, how does the volunteer feel about remaining in this position?

What else can be done to support the volunteer in this position or to move the volunteer to a new position?

Signed:

_____   _____
SUPERVISOR   VOLUNTEER (OPTIONAL)

_____   _____
DATE   DATE

Scheduled date of the next evaluation. _____

EXIT INTERVIEW QUESTIONNAIRE

We are always striving to improve the performance of our volunteer management system. As one of our volunteers, we would appreciate your help in identifying areas where we might do better. Please be as complete and honest as you can in answering the following questions—all of the information collected will be kept strictly confidential, but it it will help to ensure that others who volunteer receive the best possible treatment.

How long did you volunteer with us? _____

Types of volunteer positions held:

1. _____
2. _____
3. _____
4. _____

Why are you leaving? (Check all that apply)

❑ Job accomplished   ❑ Moving house   ❑ Need a change
❑ Didn't like the post I was given   ❑ Didn't feel well used   ❑ New paid job
❑ Can no longer meet time commitments
❑ Other: _____

What did you like best about volunteering with us?
_____
_____
_____
_____

What suggestions would you make for changes or improvements in our use of volunteers?
_____
_____
_____

Overall, how would you rate your experience in volunteering with us?

TERRIBLE			AVERAGE			GREAT
1	2	3	4	5	6	7

Please return this form to:

Name: _____
Address: _____

APPENDIX C
BIBLIOGRAPHY

◆ **The following is a US reading list on volunteering compiled by the authors of this text. Reference is made to some of the titles in the text.**

Adams, C., 'Communication and Motivation within the Superior-Subordinate Dyad: Testing the Conventional Wisdom of Volunteer Management,' *Journal of Applied Communication Research*, (Fall 1988).

Allen, K. and Harrison, S., *Families Volunteer: A Workbook for Involving Families* (Washington: The National Volunteer Center) 1983.

Amenta, M.M., 'Death, Anxiety, Purpose in Life and Duration of Service in Hospice Volunteers,' *Psychological Reports*, (June 1984).

Bigler, N., 'Keeping 4-H Volunteer Leaders,' *Journal of Extension*, (Summer 1985).

Brainard, S., 'Creating an Organizational Climate to Motivate Volunteers,' *Journal of Arts Management and the Law*, (Summer 1987).

Brown, E. and Zahrly, J., 'Commitment and Tenure of Highly Skilled Volunteers: Management Issues in a Nonprofit Agency,' Working Paper No. 12. San Francisco: Institute for Nonprofit Organization Management, University of San Francisco (February 1990).

Brown, E. and Zahrly, J., 'Nonmonetary Rewards for Skilled Volunteer Labor: A Look at Crisis Intervention Volunteers,' *Nonprofit and Voluntary Sector Quarterly*, (1989).

Brown, K., *Keys to Making a Volunteer Program Work*, (Richmond, CA: Arden Publications) 1982.

Brudney, J. and Duncombe, W., 'An Economic Evaluation of Paid, Volunteer, and Mixed Staffing Options for Public Services,' *Public Administration Review*, (1992).

Brudney, J., *Fostering Volunteer Programs in the Public Sector* (San Francisco: Jossey-Bass) 1990.

Byrne, R. and Caskey, F., 'For Love or Money: What Motivates Volunteers?', *Journal of Extension*, (Fall 1985).

Carson, E., 'The Charitable Activities of Black Americans,' *Review of Black Political Economy*, (1987).

Chambre, S., 'Recruiting Black and Hispanic Volunteers: A Qualitative Study of Organizations' Experiences,' *Journal of Volunteer Administration*, (1982).

Chambre, S., *Good Deeds in Old Age: Volunteering by the New Leisure Class*, (Lexington, MA: Lexington Books) 1987.

Chambre, S., 'Job Sharing for Volunteers', *Voluntary Action Leadership* (Summer 1989).

Chambre, S., *Responding to Uncertainty by Bearing Witness: Volunteering as Collective Behavior in the AIDS Epidemic, 1981-88,* (New York: Center for the Study of Philanthropy) 1990.

Clary, E.G., and Miller, J., 'Socialization and Situational Influences on Sustained Voluntarism,' *Child Development*, (December 1986).

Clemes, H. and Beam, R., *Self-Esteem,* (New York: Putnam) 1981.

Collins, G., Barth, J., and Zrimec, G., 'Recruiting and Retaining Alcoholics Anonymous Volunteers in a Hospital Alcoholism Program,' *Hospital and Community Psychiatry*, (1981).

Colomy, P., Chen, H. and Andrews, G., 'Situational Facilities and Volunteer Work,' *Journal of Volunteer Administration*, (Winter 1987-88).

Conway, J., 'Young, Urban Professionals Work to Show New York Cares,' *Wall Street Journal*, (June 21, 1990).

Cook, A., 'Retiring the Volunteer: Facing Reality when Service is No Longer Possible,' *Journal of Volunteer Administration* (Summer 1992).

Cooley, E., 'Volunteers as Part of Family Support Services for Families of Developmentally Disabled Members,' *Education and Training in Mental Retardation*, (September 1987).

Dailey, Robert, 'Understanding Organizational Commitment for Volunteers: Empirical and Managerial Implications,' *Journal of Voluntary Action Research*, (January-March 1986).

Distefano, M.K., and Pryer, M.W., 'Ability, Training Performance and Demographic Factors in Voluntary Turnover among Psychiatric Aides,' *Psychological Reports*, (October 1982).

Ellis, S. and Noyes, K., *By the People: A History of Americans as Volunteers.* (2nd ed. (San Francisco: Jossey-Bass) 1990.

Ellis, S., *From the Top Down: The Executive Role in Volunteer Program Success.* (Philadelphia: Energize, Inc.) 1986.

Fels, L., Getting Started: Establishing a Volunteer Program, (Vancouver, BC : Vancouver Volunteer Centre).

Field, D., and Johnson, I., 'Satisfaction and Change: A Survey of Volunteers in a Hospice Organisation,' *Social Science and Medicine* (June 1993).

Fischer, L. and Schaffer, K., *Older Volunteers: A Guide to Research and Practice.* (Newbury Park, Calif.: Sage Publications) 1993.

Fisher, J. and Cole, K., *Leadership and Management of Volunteer Programs: A Guide for Volunteer Administrators.* (San Francisco: Jossey-Bass) 1993.

Gidron, B., 'Predictors of Retention and Turnover among Service Volunteer Workers,' *Journal of Social Science Research*, (Fall 1984).

Gidron, B., 'Sources of Job Satisfaction among Service Volunteers,' *Journal of Voluntary Action Research*, (January-March 1983).

Glasser, W., *Control Theory* (New York: Harper and Row) 1984.

Graff, L., *By Definition: Policies for Volunteer Programs,* (Ontario: Volunteer Ontario) 1993.

Gregory, N. and Schueck, P., 'One Job, Two Contented Workers,' *Voluntary Action Leadership* (Winter 1988-89).

Grieshop, J., 'How Art Thou Motivated? Let Me Count the Ways!' , in *Motivating Volunteers*, (Vancouver: Volunteer Centre) 1985.

Griggs, J., editor, *Simple Acts of Kindness: Volunteering in the Age of AIDS*, (New York,NY: United Hospital Fund) 1989.

Halperin, S. and Merenda, D., *Noble Allies: Volunteers in the Schools,* (Washington, DC: Council for Basic Education) 1986.

Hanawi, L., 'An Interactive Model for Volunteerism,' Working Paper No. 14, Institute for Nonprofit Organization Management, University of San Francisco, July 1990.

Heidrich, K., *Working with Volunteers in Employee Services and Recreation Programs,* (Champaign: Sagamore Publishing) 1990.

Henderson, K., 'Are Volunteers Worth Their Weight in Gold?' , *Parks and Recreation*, (1988).

Henderson, Karla., 'Volunteerism as Leisure,' *Journal of Voluntary Action Research*, (January-March 1984).

Hipp, L. and Davis, D., 'Using Experiential Techniques in Hospice Volunteer Training,' *Journal of Volunteer Administration*, (1987).

Hodgkinson, V. and Weitzman, M., *Giving and Volunteering in the United States.* (Washington, D.C.: Independent Sector,)1988.

Hodgkinson, V. and Weitzman, M., *Giving and Volunteering in the United States.* (Washington, D.C.: Independent Sector) 1992.

Hollander, G., *Volunteer Management: Development and Maintenance of Volunteer Programs in AIDS Service Organizations,* (Washington, DC: National Aids Network) 1988.

Hollwitz, J. and Wilson, C., 'New Directions in Volunteer Selection: The Case for Structured Interviewing,' in B. Long and J. Long, (eds.), *Worn Paths and Unbroken Trails: The Volunteer Movement at the Turning Point,* (Walla Walla, Wash.: MBA Publishing) 1989.

Ilsley, P., *Enhancing the Volunteer Experience.* (San Francisco: Jossey-Bass) 1990.

Ilsley, P. and Niemi, A., *Recruiting and Training Volunteers,* (New York: McGraw-Hill) 1981.

Jenner, J.P., 'Organizational Commitment among Women Volunteers: Meaning and Measurement,' *Psychological Reports,* (June 1984).

Keyton, J., Wilson, G. and Geiger, C., 'Improving Volunteer Commitment to Organizations,' *Journal of Volunteer Administration,* (Summer 1990).

Lafer, B., 'Predicting Performance and Persistence in Hospice Volunteers,' *Psychological Reports,* (October 1989).

Lafer, B. and Craig, S., 'The Evaluation of Hospice Home Care Volunteers,' *Hspice Journal* (1993).

Lammers, J., 'Attitudes, Motives, and Demographical Predictors of Volunteer Commitment and Service Duration,' *Journal of Social Service Research,* (1991).

Latting, J., 'Motivational Differences between Black and White Volunteers,' *Nonprofit and Voluntary Sector Quarterly,* (1990).

Lucas, W., 'Cost Savings from Volunteer Services: A Research Note,' *Journal of Offender Counseling Services and Rehabilitation,* (1988).

Lynch, R., 'Preparing an Effective Recruitment Campaign,' *Voluntary Action Leadership* (Winter 1984).

Lynch, R., *Precision Management: How to Build and Lead the Winning Organization* (Seattle: Abbot Press) 1988.

Macduff, N., *Episodic Volunteering: Building the Short-Term Volunteer Program.* (Walla Walla, Wash.: MBA Associates) 1991.

Macduff, N., 'Episodic Volunteering: Reality for the Future,' *Voluntary Action Leadership* (Spring 1980).

MacKenzie, M., *Dealing with Difficult Volunteers,* (Downers Grove: Heritage Arts) 1988.

MacKenzie, M. and Moore, G., *The Group Member's Handbook,* (Downers Grove: Heritage Arts) 1993.

MacKenzie, M. and Moore, G., *The Volunteer Development Toolbox,* (Downers Grove: Heritage Arts) 1993.

Mausner, C., 'The Underlying Dynamics of Staff-Volunteer Relationships,' *Journal of Volunteer Administration,* (1988).

McCurley, S., 'How to Fire a Volunteer and Live to Tell About It,' *Grapevine,* (January/February 1993).

McCurley, S., 'Liability and Volunteer Management: Screening Volunteers,' *Grapevine,* (September/October 1991).

McCurley, S., *Recruiting Volunteers for Difficult or Long-Term Assignments.* (Downers Grove, Illinois: Heritage Arts) 1991.

McCurley, S., and Vineyard, S., *101 Ideas for Volunteer Programs,* (Downers Grove: Heritage Arts) 1986.

McCurley, S., and Vineyard, S., *101 Tips for Volunteer Recruitment,* (Downers Grove: Heritage Arts) 1988.

McCurley, S., *Recruiting Volunteers for Difficult or Long-Term Assignments,* (Downers Grove: Heritage Arts) 1990.

McCurley, S., *Volunteer Management Forms,* (Downers Grove: Heritage Arts) 1988.

McCurley, S., *Volunteer Management Policies,* (Downers Grove: Heritage Arts) 1990.

Miller, L., 'Understanding the Motivation of Volunteers: An Examination of Personality Differences and Characteristics of Volunteers' Paid Employment,' *Journal of Voluntary Action Research,* (1985).

Miller, L., Powell, G. and Seltzer, J., 'Determinants of Turnover Among Volunteers,' *Human Relations,* (1990).

Morrow-Howell, N., and Mui, A., 'Elderly Volunteers: Reasons for Initiating and Terminating Service,' *Journal of Gerontological Social Work,* (1987).

Nestor, L., 'Hispanic Volunteers – Tapping a New Volunteer Market,' *Voluntary Action Leadership,* (Fall 1984).

Nestor, L., 'Managing Cultural Diversity in Volunteer Organizations,' *Voluntary Action Leadership,* (Summer 1991).

Pearce, N., *Volunteers: The Organizational Behavior of Unpaid Workers* (New York: Routledge) 1993.

Pierucci, J. and Noel, R., 'Duration of Participation of Correctional Volunteers as a Function of Personal and Situational Variables,' *Journal of Community Psychology,* (1980).

Pinder, C., 'Needs, Cognitive Factors, and the Motivation to Volunteer,' in *Motivating Volunteers* (Vancouver: Volunteer Centre) 1985.

Rogers, J., 'Maintaining Volunteer Participation in Adult Literacy Programs,' *Lifelong Learning,* (October 1984).

Rubin, A. and Thorelli, I.M., 'Egoistic Motives and Longevity of Participation by Social Service Volunteers,' *Journal of Applied Behavioural Science,* (1984).

Saxon, J. and Sawyer, H., 'A Systematic Approach for Volunteer Assignment and Retention,' *Journal of Volunteer Administration,* (1984).

Scheier, I., 'Staff Nonsupport of Volunteers: A New Look at an Old Failure,' *Voluntary Action Leadership.,* (Fall 1977).

Scheier, I., *When Everyone's a Volunteer: The Effective Functioning of All-Volunteer Groups.* (Philadelphia: Energize, Inc.), 1992.

Scheier, I., 'Improving Volunteer Motivation through Job Design' , in *Motivating Volunteers* (Vancouver: Volunteer Centre) 1985.

Scheier, I., *Building Work that Satisfies: Staff as Well as Volunteers* (Santa Fe,NM: Center for Creative Community) 1988.

Scheier, I., *Building Work that Satisfies: Volunteers and the Window of Work* (Santa Fe,NM: Center for Creative Community)1988.

Scheier, I., *Exploding the Big Banquet Theory of Volunteer Recognition: An Incendiary Analysis* (Santa Fe,NM: Center for Creative Community)1988.

Scheier, I., *Exploring Volunteer Space,* (Santa Fe,NM: Center for Creative Community)1980.

Scheier, I., *Orienting Staff to Volunteers,* (Santa Fe,NM: Center for Creative Community)1972.

Scheier, I., *So You Still Want to Win with Staff,* (Santa Fe,NM: Center for Creative Community)1988.

Silver, N., *At the Heart,* (Pleasanton: Valley Volunteer Center) 1988.

Skillingstad, C., 'Training Supervisors of Volunteers,' *Journal of Volunteer Administration,* (1989).

Smith, E. and Grotheil., 'Successful Foster Parent Recruiting: A Voluntary Agency Effort,' *Child Welfare,* (March-April 1988).

Snider, A., 'The Dynamic Tension: Professionals and Volunteers,' *Journal of Extension,* (Fall 1985).

Unger, L, 'Effect of Actual and Perceived Availability of Time on Voluntarism,' *Perceptual and Motor Skills,* (October 1987).

Utterback, J. and Heyman, S., 'An Examination of Methods in the Evaluation of Volunteer Programs,' *Evaluation and Program Planning,* (1984).

Vineyard, S., *Beyond Banquets, Plaques and Pins: Creative Ways to Recognize Volunteers.* (Downers Grove: Heritage Arts), 2nd edition, 1989.

Vineyard, S., *Evaluating Volunteers Programs and Events.* (Downers Grove: Heritage Arts), 1988.

Vineyard, S., *Megatrends for Volunteerism,* (Downers Grove: Heritage Arts) 1993.

Vineyard, S., *Secrets of Motivation: How to Get and Keep Volunteers and Staff,* (Downers Grove: Heritage Arts) 1990.

Vineyard, S. and McCurley, S., eds., *Managing Volunteer Diversity,* (Downers Grove: Heritage Arts)1989.

Watts, A. and Edwards, P., 'Recruiting and Retaining Human Service Volunteers: An Empirical Analysis,' *Journal of Voluntary Action Research,* (July-September 1983).

Williams, R., 'Receptivity to Persons with Mental Retardation: A Study of Volunteer Interest,' *American Journal of Mental Retardation,* (November 1987).

Wilson, M., *The Effective Management of Volunteer Programs.* (Boulder, Colorado: Volunteer Management Associates), 1976.

Wright, B., 'Some Notes on Recruiting and Retaining Minority Volunteers,' *Voluntary Action Leadership,* 1 (Winter 1992).

FURTHER READING

Publications available from the Volunteer Centre UK Carriage Row, 18 Eversholt Street, London, NW1 1BU 071 383 9888

WORKING WITH VOLUNTEERS HANDBOOKS

Support Jill Pitkeathley
Training Lisa Conway
Recruitment and Selection Bob Mackenzie

Good Practice Guides

Volunteers in the Driving Seat Ruth Horton
Making the Right Choice Angela Witcher
Protecting Volunteers Cressida Wasserman and Angela Witcher
Volunteers First: A Guide to Employment Practice Angela Witcher and Angie McDonough
Guidelines for Relations between Volunteers and Paid Workers in the Health and Personal Social Services
The Promotion of Volunteering: A value base for voluntary action in the 1990s

The Impact of Contracts on Volunteers Giles Darvill
All Expenses Paid: Answers to some Questions about Paying Expenses to Volunteers
Local Government and Volunteers Giles Darvill
Working it Out: Some Guidelines for Project Organisers Matt Doyle and Ian Mocroft

Voluntary Action Research Papers

The 1991 National Survey of Voluntary Activity in the United Kingdom
Volunteering Matters: Developments in Volunteering 1992-1994 Ruth Horton (new publication)
Volunteering Today: An Action Guide for Volunteer Organisers Rodney Hedley
Criminal Records Checks within the Voluntary Sector: An Evaluation of the Pilot Schemes Judith Unell
Understanding Management Committees: A Look at Volunteer Committee Members Rodney Hedley and Colin Rochester
Making It Happen! Involving Black Volunteers
On Volunteering: A Qualitative Research Study of Images, Motivations and Experiences, 1990

Time is Money: The Costs of Volunteering in Britain Today, 1991
Martin Knapp
The Involvement of Volunteers in Rural Areas of England, 1991
Encouraging Signs? A report of a survey of Black Participation in Voluntary Organisations, 1991
Volunteering in HIV and AIDS Organisations: A Report of a Survey, 1991
A Directory of Research into Voluntary Action 1989-1991
Volunteers and the Contract Culture: Voluntary Action Research Third Series Paper by Rodney Hedley and Justin Davis Smith (new publication)
Paid to Volunteer: The Extent of Paying Volunteers in the 1990s Sarah Blacksell and David R Phillips (new publication).

Books on Specific Themes

Managing Volunteers Mark Rankin
Step by Step: A Guide to Volunteers Fund-raising Edited by Ruth Horton
A Guide to Employee Volunteering
The Gentle Art of Listening: Counselling Skills for Volunteers Janet K Ford and Philippa Merriman
Volunteering and Society: Principles and Practice Edited by Rodney Hedley and Justin Davis Smith
Volunteers on Management Committees Rodney Hedley and Colin Rochester

RESOURCE PUBLICATIONS

Training Resource Packs

Training Resource Pack 1: Volunteers in Community Care Services

Resources for Employee Volunteering

Employees in the Community: A Handbook for Action Jo Paton
Understanding Employee Volunteering Jo Paton
Making the Most of Employee Community Involvement Jo Paton
Employee Volunteering Guide No 1: Surveys and How to Make a Success of Them Jo Paton

Resources for Environmental Volunteering

The Environmental Volunteering Handbook Jonathan Pinkney-Baird
Volunteer Management Guidelines

Reading Lists

Active Citizenship Reading List
Community Care Reading List
Government Policy and Volunteering Reading List
Recruitment Reading List
Volunteer Response to Civil Emergencies Reading List
Environmental Reading List
Volunteers in Museums and Art Galleries Reading List

Information Sheets

Volunteering Opportunities UK
Getting Started
Volunteers' Welfare Benefits and Taxation
Volunteers: recruitment, training and support
Finding out about volunteering
Ceefax
Volunteering opportunities overseas

Publications Available from Directory of Social Change Radius Works, Back Lane, London, NW3 1HL 071 431 1817

Directory of Volunteering and Employment Opportunities Jan Brownfoot and Frances Wilks
How to Work for a Charity On a Paid or Voluntary Basis Jan Brownfoot and Frances Wilks
Just about Managing Effective Management for Voluntary Organisations and Community Groups Sandy Adirondack
Planning Together The Art of Effective Teamwork George Gawlinski and Lois Graessle
The Trustee Organiser Ring binder fact file (1993)
The Effective Trustee Basic Guides - Parts 1, 2 & 3 (1993/1994) Kevin Ford
How to be a Better Trustee Training Packs - Parts1, 2 &3 Kevin Ford

ACTION: EMPLOYEES IN THE COMMUNITY
8 Stratton Street, London, W1X 5FD Tel No: 071 629 2209

BUSINESS IN THE COMMUNITY (BITC)
8 Stratton Street, London, W1X 5FD Tel No: 071 629 1600

COMMUNITY SERVICE VOLUNTEERS (CVS)
237 Pentonville Road, London N1 9NJ Tel No: 071 278 6601

COMMUNITY DEVELOPMENT FOUNDATION (CDF)
60 Highbury Grove, London, N5 2AG Tel No: 071 226 5375

DIRECTORY OF SOCIAL CHANGE RADIUS WORKS,
Back Lane, London, NW3 1HL Tel No: 071 435 8171

NATIONAL ASSOCIATION OF VOLUNTEER BUREAUX (NAVB) St Peter's
College, College Road, Saltley, Birmingham, B8 3TE Tel No: 021 327 0265

NATIONAL ASSOCIATION OF COUNCILS FOR VOLUNTARY SERVICE
(NACVS) 3rd Floor, Arundel Court, 177 Arundel Street, Sheffield, S1 2NU
Tel No: 0742 786 636

NATIONAL COUNCIL FOR VOLUNTARY ORGANISATIONS (NCVO) Regents
Wharf, 8 All Saints Street, London, N1 9RL Tel No: 071 713 6161

NATIONAL YOUTH AGENCY
17-23 Albion Street, Leicester, LE1 6GD Tel No: 0533 471 200

NORTHERN IRELAND COUNCIL OF VOLUNTARY ACTION 127 Ormeau Road,
Belfast, BT7 1SH Tel No: 0232 321224

NORTHERN IRELAND VOLUNTEER DEVELOPMENT AGENCY: Annsgate
House, 70-74 Anns Street, Belfast, BT1 4EH Tel No: 0232 236 100

SCOTTISH COUNCIL FOR VOLUNTARY ORGANISATIONS
18-19 Claremont Crescent, Edinburgh, EH7 4QD Tel No: 031 556 3882

WALES COUNCIL FOR VOLUNTARY ACTION
Llys Ifor, Crescent Road, Caerphilly, Mid Glamorgan, CF8 1XL
Tel No: 0222 869224

VOLUNTEER CENTRE UK
Carriage Row, 183 Eversholt Street, London, NW1 1BU Tel No: 071 388 9888

VOLUNTEER DEVELOPMENT SCOTLAND
80 Murray Place, Stirling, FX8 2BX Tel No: 0786 479593